Residential Child Care

of related interest

Effective Ways of Working with Children and their Families
Edited by Malcolm Hill
ISBN 1 85302 619 0 pb

Welfare and Culture in Europe
Towards a New Paradigm in Social Policy
Edited by Prue Chamberlayne, Andrew Cooper, Richard Freeman and Michael Rustin
ISBN 1 85302 700 6 pb

State Child Care Practice
Looking After Children?
Carol Hayden, Jim Goddard, Sarah Gorin and Niki Van Der Spek
ISBN 1 85302 670 0 pb

The Adoption Experience
Families who Give Children a Second Chance
Ann Morris
ISBN 1 85302 783 9 pb

Issues in Foster Care
The Personal, the Professional and the Organisational
Edited by Grey Kelly and Robbie Gilligan
ISBN 1 85302 465 1 pb

Children's Homes Revisited
David Berridge and Isabelle Brodie
ISBN 1 85302 565 8 pb

Young People Leaving Care
Life After the Children Act 1989
Bob Broad
ISBN 1 85302 412 0 pb

Troubles of Children and Adolescents
Edited by Ved Varma
ISBN 1 85302 323 X pb

Social Work with Children and Families
Getting into Practice
Ian Butler and Gwenda Roberts
ISBN 1 85302 365 5 pb

Lesbian and Gay Fostering and Adoption
Extraordinary Yet Ordinary
Edited by Stephen Hicks and Janet McDermott
ISBN 1 85302 600 X pb

Children in Need and Voluntary Sector Services
The Northern Ireland Approach
Kerry O'Halloran, Arthur Williamson and Goretti Horgan
ISBN 1 85302 712 X pb

Residential Child Care

International Perspectives on Links with Families and Peers

Edited by Mono Chakrabarti and Malcolm Hill

Jessica Kingsley Publishers
London and Philadelphia

The right of the contributors to be identified as authors of this work has been asserted by them in accordance with the Copyright, Designs and Patents Act 1988.

First published in the United Kingdom in 2000 by
Jessica Kingsley Publishers Ltd,
116 Pentonville Road, London
N1 9JB, England
and
325 Chestnut Street,
Philadelphia PA 19106, USA.

www.jkp.com

© Copyright 2000 Jessica Kingsley Publishers

Library of Congress Cataloging in Publication Data
Residential child care : links with families and peers / edited by
Mono Chakrabarti and Malcolm Hill.
   p.   cm.
  Includes bibliographical references and index.
  ISBN 1-85302-687-5 (alk. paper)
  1. Children--Institutional care--Great Britain. 2. Foster home care--Great Britain.
3. Foster children--Great Britain--Family relationship. 4. Foster children--Social
networks--Great Britain. 5. Child welfare--Great Britain. I. Chakrabarti, Mono.
II. Hill, Malcolm.
HV866.G7R47 1999   99-41647
362.73'0941--dc21   CIP

British Library Cataloguing in Publication Data
Residential child care : links with families and peers
  1. Children - Institutional care 2. Children - Family relationships
3. Problem children - Family relationships
I. Chakrabarti, Mono II. Hill, Malcolm
362.7'32
ISBN 1 85302 687 5

ISBN 1 85302 687 5

Printed and Bound in Great Britain by
Athenaeum Press, Gateshead, Tyne and Wear

Contents

Preface

In September 1996, over 450 people from all the five continents came together in Glasgow, Scotland, for three days to discuss and share ideas about all aspects of residential child care. This Conference, titled *Dreams and Realities*, was organised by Meg Lindsay, Director of the Centre for Residential Child Care in Glasgow. With encouragement and support from Meg Lindsay and other colleagues, the editors have been able to put together a number of workshop papers in this volume. We hope that the papers included will be of interest and use to all those working in the field of residential child care.

Our thanks go to Irene Bloomfield of the University of Glasgow for her helpful and perceptive comments in relation to the first two chapters.

We are especially grateful to Meg Lindsay for organising such a successful conference and for facilitating the developments of this publication.

We wish to record our sincere thanks and gratitude to all the contributors.

CHAPTER I

The Residential Child Care Context

Malcolm Hill

Introduction

Each year a small proportion of children and young people leave their families and are admitted to children's homes. These are among some of our most deprived and troubled citizens, who usually have very difficult family backgrounds. It is the responsibility of residential staff and carers, acting on behalf of society at large, to promote these children's well-being and to minimise the negative consequences of separation.

When charitable and public children's homes were first built on a large scale, they were typically seen as offering refuge from what were seen to be the defective or immoral influences of their families. Just like hospitals for the physically and mentally ill, large establishments were built to house mainly inner city children in the suburbs and countryside miles away from the contamination of their origins (Heywood 1978; Hill, Murray and Rankin 1991). Indeed for decades some children were shipped overseas for a complete fresh start. Nowadays, in the West at least, the world of residential child care is vastly different from that of the Victorian era. Yet a key issue remains – what should be the relationship between children in public care and their families and social networks? On the one hand, current child care principles have increasingly emphasised respect for children's family ties and the need for carers and professionals to work 'in partnership' with parents. On the other hand, increased awareness of child abuse or maltreatment over the last 30 years has highlighted the risks which parents and other household members can pose to their children. The official responses to child abuse, which have come to be known collectively as child protection, have become major routes into residential care (Lindsey 1994). Drug misuse leading to abuse and neglect has been a major factor, especially in North America (Hogan 1998).

This book sets out to explore the nature and significance of inclusive or exclusive approaches to the families of children in residential care. Since the forms and purposes of children's homes and kindred establishments have changed markedly in recent years, the present chapter explores the current context of residential child care. This will be considered mainly from a UK perspective, but with references to trends elsewhere.

In the next chapter we shall examine the nature and extent of contact between children in homes and their families and the role of staff in relation to family contacts and family problems. This will lead on to an overview of the place of families in theories of residential child care and the rationale for an inclusive orientation. First, though, it will be helpful to discuss briefly matters of terminology.

The meaning and scope of residential child care

For many years, the phrase 'in care' was used in Britain to refer to children residing in foster homes or children's homes under public auspices. Somewhat confusingly, in the United States the term foster care has a similar meaning, covering both residential care and foster family care. Under the influence of the Children Act 1989, new terminology was introduced to England and Wales in the hope that this would have less stigmatising connotations than 'in care'. Now children who stay away from their family home under the responsibility of a local authority are said to be 'looked after' by that authority. If the arrangement is made with parental agreement, then the child is 'accommodated'. These terms were introduced somewhat later in Scotland and Northern Ireland (Kelly and Pinkerton 1996; Tisdall 1996), though in Scotland 'children looked after' include those still living at home but subject to compulsory supervision by the local authority ('home supervision'). For convenience, the phrases 'in care' and 'looked after' will be used interchangeably in this chapter.

In Britain, as in most of the rest of the world, children may become 'looked after' either on a compulsory basis through a court (or equivalent) or with parental agreement, indeed often by parental request. As we shall see later, the differences between foster care and residential care in Britain are much less marked than they used to be, but essentially foster families offer care in their own homes, whereas in residential care staff are paid to look after children in a setting specially built or acquired for that purpose. According to a recent definition, a residential placement 'is a place where children live and sleep, for at least one night. As a rule the adults who look after the children will be employed for that purpose' (Department of Health 1998, p.7).

As soon as international comparisons are made, it becomes apparent that the types of institutions and their functions which are embraced in discussions of residential child care vary significantly. Differences in definition reflect in part contrasts in tradition and provision, but also different boundaries set around the concept. In particular, boarding schools and placements for young offenders may be included or excluded. Generally, private boarding schools for the wealthy are excluded, though a number of commentators have remarked on their high regard and successful outcomes compared with publicly run residential schools (Parker 1988; Kahan 1994). In Israel much less distinction is made between respected boarding provision and facilities for disadvantaged families (Levy 1994).

Many countries have separate institutions for young offenders (e.g. coming under the corrections system in North America). In Europe these have mostly become less prison-like over the years (Poso 1996) and often the great majority of young offenders who are thought by a court to require residential care are sent to mainstream children's homes. For example, in Belgium a custodial sentence should only be made when no appropriate place can be found in a youth protection home (Walgrave *et al.* 1998). Normally, hospital provision is not counted as a form of residential care, but child and adolescent psychiatric units or other kinds of children's mental health provision are sometimes included. In some parts of the world long-stay medically run residential facilities are an important component, especially for children with disabilities (Zamfir and Zamfir 1994).

Public group care for children can be the responsibility of a wide range of central and local government departments whose precise labels and coverage vary from country to country. Broadly the main systems are social welfare, education, health and youth justice systems (Ainsworth and Fulcher 1981). These in turn represent a number of general functions – social and health care, education and social control.

In North America specialist child and youth care workers are common. Most have received dedicated college training. Agencies which run residential establishments often employ specific professionals like psychologists and family therapists (Charles and Gabor 1988; Ainsworth 1997). In the UK and Ireland, most residential care staff have no formal qualification, though usually they have taken part in a certain amount of in-service agency training. They are identified as (residential) social workers (Madge 1994; Skinner 1992; Berridge and Brodie 1998). Italy and France also have many unqualified workers, whereas Germany has a particularly high proportion of staff with specialist training (over 90%). In Western Europe, many establishments employ social pedagogues and animateurs, trained in a broad range of education theories and skills embracing individual development and group processes. Further east and in parts of the developing world, medical, nursing and conventional teaching qualifications are more typical (UNICEF 1997).

Most staff are female – usually 70–80 per cent. Some countries like Sweden have made special efforts to attract more men (Madge 1994).

Types of residential child care establishment

Children looked after in public care can be placed in any of three main sectors:

- publicly run provision
- private or for-profit sector
- voluntary facilities (run by not-for-profit or non-governmental organisations).

Generally public or state facilities are run by local government, though commonly more penal establishments are run by the central or federal government (see e.g. Poso 1996). In England, the majority of residential homes are run by local authorities, with just under 10 per cent each being private and voluntary (House of Commons Health Committee 1998). In Scandinavia too, with its strong commitment to public welfare, nearly all provision is publicly run, mainly by municipalities (Barth 1992; Kemppainen 1994). When all other options have not worked, then child offenders in Finland may be placed in community homes run by the National Board of Social Welfare (as opposed to children's homes run by municipalities) (Poso 1991). The Catholic and Orthodox churches have long been major providers in Southern Europe (Agathanos-Georgopoulou 1993; Madge 1994). Similarly, up to the 1980s, religious orders were responsible for many children's homes in Ireland, but they have now mostly withdrawn from this function, leaving responsibility to the state (Gilligan 1993; Brennan 1994).

The nature of individual establishments in Britain has changed dramatically in the last 20 to 30 years, with the closure of many old buildings to be replaced by purpose-built establishments or the conversion of ordinary housing. By the 1980s the Victorian and pre-war inheritance of large institutions and residential village communities were fast moving into history. Parker (1988) noted that residential nurseries were rapidly disappearing, as it was now believed that younger children should be placed in foster care and in any case large establishments with a high staff turnover had been discredited by research (Rutter 1981). The fashion for specialist Observation and Assessment Centres was also on the wane. These were intended to identify the long-term placement needs of children in care, though in practice the desired solution was sometimes not available and children either overstayed or had to move on to other short-term placements. In 1985, Berridge classified children's homes without education on the premises into:

- family group homes
- adolescent hostels
- larger multi-purpose homes.

A further important type of residential facility were boarding schools (Community homes with education in England and Wales; List D schools in Scotland). These were used particularly, though not exclusively, for young offenders. Youngsters with emotional and behavioural difficulties were often sent to residential schools run by education rather than social services developments (Grimshaw with Berridge 1994).

During the 1990s, usage of the intermediate placements declined, with many closing, so that Berridge and Brodie (1998) concluded that provision had become polarised, with children's homes and adolescent hostels at one end of the spectrum and secure or penal measures at the other. However, in parts of the country, residential schools were still an important resource (Triseliotis *et al.* 1995), whilst the private sector had developed a number of specialist treatment centres (Department of Health 1998). The latter mainly concentrate on very difficult teenagers at some distance from their homes (Gibbs and Sinclair 1998).

It appears that a similar range of provision is to be found elsewhere in Western Europe and in North America. For example, the main facilities in Denmark (Melhbye 1993) are:

- small children's homes
- community homes with on-site education (residential schools)
- specialist treatment centres for those with particular difficulties (some privately run).

Several countries make considerable use of boarding schools for children in care (Madge 1994). Older teenagers may have access to innovative initiatives including ship or farm projects, intended to capitalise on the value of sharing exciting and possibly vocational activities (Trapp and Wolffersdorff 1991). In Canada wilderness camps serve a similar purpose and some cater for native peoples by drawing on traditional customs.

The pattern in Eastern Europe is quite different, with three main types of large institution differentiated by age and ability. These are infant homes, children's homes for older children and establishments for children with disabilities. In each type schooling is usually provided on the premises (UNICEF 1997).

To avoid repetitiveness, a number of different words and phrases will be used from now on to refer collectively to children's homes and residential schools. These include 'establishments', 'residential care', 'units' and 'centres'.

Numbers of children in residential care

In most of Western Europe the 1980s and 1990s witnessed a substantial decline in the numbers of children staying in residential care, both in absolute terms and as a proportion of those placed away from home compared with foster family care (Colton and Hellinckx 1993; Madge 1994; Vaaben 1994). From 1985 to 1995, the numbers of children living in children's homes in England more than halved (Berridge and Brodie 1998). If residential schools are ignored, the decline is even steeper (Department of Health 1998). The voluntary sector shrank from 4000 to a mere 600 places. Similarly in the Netherlands the number of children in residential care halved between the 1970s and 1990s, while Belgium and France experienced decreases of more than one-third. (West) Germany was an exception to this trend, however, with numbers remaining stable (Frommann and Trede 1994). A combination of factors help account for the accelerated retrenchment of the residential care sector since the 1970s. These include: policy and practice shifts towards preventive services; changed awareness and attitudes about children's needs; and financial considerations (Gooch 1996).

This decrease may be seen as a positive trend, indicating that community resources are now better developed and that increasingly young people are placed in residential care only when that is the preferred option. On the other hand, the shrinkage of the residential sector may reinforce its image as a residual service, a 'last resort'. Furthermore, the choice of facilities in any one area is reduced and it can be increasingly difficult to separate different types of child, for example, offenders or abusers from victims (House of Commons Health Committee 1998).

In the United States, by contrast, numbers have tended to increase, partly in response to severe drug problems in many urban areas (Downs, Costin and McFadden 1996, Waldfogel 1998). For different reasons, more children are looked after in residential care in Eastern Europe than before the ending of state communism. For example, in Romania during the five years after 1989, the numbers in residential care increased by 4500 to over 39,000, despite some growth in foster care places from about 6000 to over 8000. The main exception has been Hungary, where the residential population has significantly declined, thanks to more favourable economic circumstances and generous family assistance (UNICEF 1997).

The relative contribution of residential homes and schools for children looked after varies considerably from country to country, though precise comparisons are made difficult because of the varied inclusion in official statistics of educational provision and arrangements for young offenders, as noted above. In those countries where the residential sector has shrunk, overall numbers of children in care have also diminished, but usually the numbers of children in foster care have been largely maintained so fostering now caters for the majority of children. Conversely, where residential care remains the main sector, numbers have stayed more stable or increased.

In the UK, foster family placements now considerably outnumber residential placements (House of Commons Health Committee 1998; Scottish Office 1998). This results mainly from the marked drop in the use of residential care, since the numbers of foster homes have remained steady (Triseliotis, Sellick and Short 1995). Some authorities reduced their own stock of children's homes to few or none. They have continued to make a small number of residential placements in voluntary and private establishments, which can result in high expense for the council and a substantial distance between group home and family for the children (Cliffe with Berridge 1992; Packman and Hall 1998). Whilst both the number and proportion of children in care who are placed residentially has diminished considerably, it remains the case that most adolescents in care will experience a residential placement at some point (Bullock, Little and Millham 1993a; Triseliotis *et al.* 1995).

A similar pattern is evident in Scandinavia, but in Southern Europe fostering services are much less developed, so that over three-quarters of children in care are in residential establishments (Madge 1994). Within Western Europe, Spain has the highest proportion of children in residential care – 88 per cent in the early 1990s (Colton and Hellinckx 1993). Even in Germany, about 60 per cent of children in care are placed in non-family settings (Frommann and Trede 1994).

Outside the West, a mixture of cultural or political traditions and economic conditions usually mean that foster family placements beyond the kin network are little developed so that residential placements predominate. This is very much the case in Eastern Europe, though some Western NGOs have helped set up small family placement schemes (Dickens and Watts 1997; Pringle 1998; Sellick 1998). A study of nearly 900 children in care in Hong Kong revealed that three-quarters were in residential placements.

About 40 per cent were in residential crèches or nurseries catering for children up to the age of six years (Tam and Ho 1993).

Unit size

Size is a significant feature of children's homes, since it has direct consequences on children's experiences and also affects social perceptions. Generally, the smaller the unit, the more scope for personalised care and planning; whereas larger establishments are difficult to organise without having standard arrangements. The intensity of adult–child and child–child relationships is likely to be affected, and the nature of group identifications will be different. Big premises are visibly 'special' and separate, so tend to evoke more stigmatising remarks and reputation from the surrounding community. Large establishments will usually have economies of scale, although that will be influenced by staff ratios. Of course, many big establishments are divided into smaller units.

Children's homes and schools have always varied greatly in size. Many nineteenth-century establishments housed one hundred or more children, often in barrack-like conditions. More enlightened philanthropists established smaller cottages intended to approximate typical family households. During the 1950s family group homes became common in Britain and the USA, with perhaps 8–10 children looked after by resident houseparents, usually a married couple (Dinnage and Pringle 1967; Kadushin and Martin 1988). These were seen to have both emotional benefits for children and to be less costly than alternatives, but they could be ill-suited to the needs of children with very challenging behaviour (Holman 1996). At this time, many large homes and schools from earlier eras continued in use, too.

From the 1960s onwards the professionalisation of residential staff and a reconceptualisation of residential care away from imitation of families were associated with the creation of 'medium-sized' establishments, housing 30 to 40 children overall, although often homes were subdivided into units for fewer children. While some of these survive, the general trend in the 1990s has been towards much smaller units housing fewer than ten children, with the intention of providing more individualised care (Madge 1994). It is hoped that units of this size will finally lay to rest certain institutionalised practices such as 'batch' activities, routines and meals, identifiable buildings and transport, and shared rooms.

The average children's home in the UK now has seven residents (Department of Health 1998) – though residential schools are larger. With some homes caring for as few as two or three children, a growing though perhaps superficial resemblance to foster care is apparent. The key difference is that staff do not live on the premises and work shifts. Whereas formerly heads of homes usually lived in, as did a proportion of other staff, this is now rare. One result of these changes is that staff may well outnumber children (Berridge and Brodie 1998), with significant consequences not only for attention, but also for the balance between staff and child power and cultures. In their recent study, Brown *et al.* (1998) found little evidence for strong resident counter-cultures, which were a feature of the larger institutions of the past.

Similar trends are apparent elsewhere, though with differing timing and scale. In Denmark homes of over 50 children have always been rare. However, recent new buildings have been smaller than before, catering for fewer than ten children, often with more of an age spread than formerly since the numbers in any one locality no longer justify having units dedicated to particular age bands (Plasvig 1991; Vaaben 1994). Policy and practice in the Netherlands and Ireland has been directed to small units in or near the neighbourhoods of origin of the residents (van der Ploeg 1993; Gilligan 1993; Brennan 1994). Often institutions for young offenders have also become more intimate, with a corresponding emphasis on treatment rather than regimentation, as in Finland (Poso 1991).

For children in many parts of the world, the opportunity to live in small homely units with highly personalised care remains a forlorn dream. For much of the post-war period, Eastern Europe was insulated from the trend to smaller establishments. Political ideals favoured communal facilities. The socialist commitment to state provision supported the development of many large collectivised long-stay institutions, typically housing from 150 to 600 children. Many staff were unqualified. Daily routines were regimented. The stress was on medical care and education, with little attention to social and emotional needs. Planning and encouragement of family contact were rare. These homes, where many children spent their entire childhood, were a world apart. Juvenile offenders were often housed in harsh, prison-like institutions (UNICEF 1997). In some areas, notably Hungary, during the 1980s there was a trend towards more family-based models, either by subdividing the large buildings into family groups or by renting outhouses (Cseres 1994). However, the average size of children's homes in East Germany actually increased in the 1970s and 1980s, so that over a hundred children was quite common (Colla-Muller 1993).

Ideological reasons were less evident in Southern Europe, but here the impact of concerns about large institutions was also much weaker than in Western Europe. Thus in the late 1980s, half of Greek children's homes housed over fifty children (Agathanos-Georgopoulou 1993). A recent ethnographic study in Portugal took place in a home with over a hundred children of all ages and including some adults (Aarre 1998).

In many developing countries large institutions remain the norm, especially where finance does not allow for more intensive care. Hong Kong, as a former British colony, was influenced by Western ideas, but has retained many traditional forms of care. Several children's homes cater for over a hundred children each. Unlike the situation in Europe, it is pre-school children who are most likely to be placed in establishments of a hundred children or more, where babies lie untended in rows of cots. Government policy in the 1990s to set up family group homes with about eight children of mixed ages has mainly affected school-age children (Bagley, Po-Chee and O'Brian 1997).

Functions of residential care

The changes in the forms of residential care just described both reflect and result in alterations in their functions. Beedell observed in 1970 that: 'The essential character of residential work for children is that it takes over a more or less substantial part of responsibility for "parenting"' (p.17). It remains the case in many parts of the world that children's homes do mostly expect to take on a quasi-parental role, assuming responsibility not only for daily care and education, but also for key directions and decisions in the child's life. Ideally this should entail not only promoting children's health and physical well-being, but also nurturing their full potential and personal integrity (Beedell 1970).

In most Western societies, in contrast, children who need long-term or permanent substitute parenting are now usually fostered or adopted. Children in residential care tend to stay for relatively short periods, though this can still amount to several years. They often retain a strong family loyalty and, one way or another, most return directly or gravitate gradually back to their families of origin (Bullock, Little and Millham 1993a). In the next chapter we shall see what this means precisely in terms of contact and continuity of relationships, but here it suffices to note that a consequence of this more temporary separation from the family is that the role taken on by residential care is more partial and in some senses more shared than in traditional long-stay establishments.

The Wagner Report of 1988 identified five main functions for children's residential care:

- respite care
- care and control

- specialised treatment
- preparation for permanent placement
- keeping sibling groups together.

The first three represent roles adopted to help children return to their home family and community as quickly as possible. Respite care means giving parents a break from accumulated stresses, perhaps associated with illness. Increasingly it also involves the mutual need or wish for teenagers and their parents in conflict to have a break from each other and regroup. This overlaps with care and control functions in relation to difficulties which may be confined to family relationships, but often manifest themselves in problems with schooling or law-breaking. Also some children are in residential homes because they have been abused in their original family and do not want to move to another family or find it difficult to do so. In such circumstances, their needs can encompass good quality care, the nurturing of relationships, in-depth therapeutic treatment and special education (Brown *et al.* 1998).

The last two functions identified by Wagner refer to the interface between residential care and family placement. It is not always easy to find a family home able to take on a set of three or more siblings, whilst some children are in residential care awaiting and hopefully being helped to prepare for a permanent family placement. Berridge (1985) observed that another core role was to assist children to recover from a foster family breakdown.

Other trends

A number of other trends can be discerned in British and Western countries as regards the nature of resident children, length of stay and the role of residential care. This contrasts with a pattern of relatively little or piecemeal change in other parts of the world.

Madge (1994) identified common features of children in residential care in the EU. Generally boys outnumber girls. Most come from disadvantaged backgrounds and the majority of adolescents are there in part because of their behaviour problems. Many have school difficulties. Neglect and abuse are other common factors. Most children do not come from intact two-parent households, but very few are orphans.

The majority of Western countries now have a strong commitment to family care for younger children. Referring to Germany, Colla-Muller (1993) observed that over the last 20 years professionals have been reluctant to place younger children in residential care. As a result, increasingly residential care has come to be a service primarily for teenage children. Sex segregation of children is now uncommon outside the larger schools (Poso 1996; Berridge and Brodie 1998).

The reduced numbers and older age at entry mean that children tend to be admitted only when they have very serious problems. Evidence from a number of countries indicates that the proportion of children with major emotional or behavioural difficulties is high and has grown over the last decade (Bullock, Little and Millham 1993b; Van den Bergh 1994). The challenges to residential staff are correspondingly greater.

Children's homes or residential schools are now seldom intended for long-term placements and few young people stay there for lengthy periods. When Berridge (1985) carried out his study of children's homes in England in the 1980s, it was not uncommon to find children who had spent four years or more in residential care. By the time of his follow-up study a dozen years later this was rare (Berridge and Brodie 1998). Another English study revealed that over half of those placed in residential care had left within a month (Bullock, Little and Millham 1993a). Nevertheless, children not infrequently come in for a short stay but are unable to return home so that their stay extends for months or even years (Brown *et al.* 1998). When this happens in an unplanned way, this is known as 'drift'.

In the Netherlands, over a decade the average length of stay decreased from 18 months to 13 months (van der Ploeg 1993). Similarly in the United States the emphasis has been on short-term placements, with a stress on speedy reunification whenever possible (Ainsworth 1997).

In many countries, low pay, unsocial hours and stressful work conditions encourage a high turnover of staff (Madge 1994; Brown *et al.* 1998). Although generally staff in the UK have become more experienced in their task, they tend to move around, so that few have worked for a long time in the same place (Berridge and Brodie 1998). The frequent changes of staff combine with a regular movement of children to give an air of imperm-anence. In some cases, children also live through a substantial change in function, structure or location in what is ostensibly the same home.

Children's homes are not only smaller than before, but have usually been located and designed (or adapted) to facilitate closer integration with the local neighbourhood. Staff attitudes and the style of buildings and furnishings have become more open to visitors, and children will now typically attend local schools rather than a campus facility, at least if they are receiving formal education. Vecchiato (1993) described the situation in Italy: 'The 1980s witnessed a shift from viewing residential care as "autonomous communities" to the idea of them being "part of a framework of community-based services for children and families"' (p.143). Arieli (1991) observed an increased openness to the surrounding community in Israeli homes, too (see also Gluck, Chapter 7 in this volume).

Whereas in the past homes were usually built far from the presumed negative influence of home and peers, nowadays most residents of children's homes live near their home communities (Berridge and Brodie 1998; Sinclair and Gibbs 1998). This can make it easier for children to achieve continuity of schooling and network relationships. For some adolescents, though, it may be harder to avoid law-breaking activities or involvement with risky activities with peers when temptation is so near.

Does residential care work?

Public interventions are increasingly subject to scrutiny. A basic concern about residential care for children has to be – is it safe? A series of scandals have revealed instances of physical and sexual abuse which have rightly alarmed the public and politicians (Levy and Kahan 1991; Berridge and Brodie 1996; Marshall, Jamieson and Finlayson 1999). These led to measures to improve recruitment, promote conditions which inhibit aggression, increase the visibility of care and encourage children to assert their rights (Kahan 1994; Kent 1998). As far as can be judged, abuse by care staff is the exception rather than the rule, but the need for constant vigilance is clear.

It is also common nowadays to ask of residential care, as of other interventions, does it work? (Alderson *et al.* 1996; Sellick and Thoburn 1996). This apparently simple question does not necessarily have an easy answer. We need to specify the criteria for success, take account of the baseline circumstances and development of children, indicate which alternatives residential care may be compared with, and so on. Further, as we have seen, residential care takes many forms and caters for many children, so that impact and outcomes can depend on the type of establishment, the kind of child and the particular match of the two.

Research evidence from the 1940s and 1950s established that children are likely to suffer emotionally, socially and intellectually if they are brought up in large institutions with little or only episodic personal affection and care (Rutter 1981; Madge 1994). Fortunately, establishments of that type no longer exist in most of the West, though as we have seen they are still quite common elsewhere. Television images of Romanian 'orphanages' and Chinese 'dying rooms' showed that extreme ill-treatment can still occur in such settings, although neglect and deprivation are probably more typical than malicious abuse. Not long ago, it was reported that children in Greek homes experienced rigid daily routines and rules, and many did not feel emotionally close to their carers (Agathanos-Georgopoulou 1993)

As regards children brought up in the medium-sized provision of the 1960s and 1970s in the West, studies showed that children who spent long periods in residential care still tended to do poorly on average compared with their peers, though some did well (Tizard 1977; Triseliotis and Russell 1984). Positive educational experiences and close attachment to a supportive carer were associated with better outcomes (Quinton and Rutter 1988).

When it comes to 'modern' residential care, the picture is more positive. Given their original family circumstances, it is only to be expected that the great majority of those in residential care have below-average scores on most developmental dimensions – both at entry and subsequently (Triseliotis *et al.* 1995; Sinclair and Gibbs 1998). However, allowing for the usually low base of educational achievement or emotional and social adjustment, most usually do show considerable progress during their stay. Only a minority experience little improvement or indeed regress (Bullock, Little and Milham 1993b; Hill *et al.* 1996; Department of Health 1998). In research carried out in England and Scotland during the early 1990s, feedback from social workers, parents and young people revealed high levels of satisfaction for over three-quarters of placements (Triseliotis *et al.* 1995). A number of studies in the UK using a range of outcome criteria have indicated that residential care performs just as well as foster care, when children of similar age and initial difficulty are compared (Millham *et al.* 1986; Rowe, Hundleby and Garnett 1989; Berridge 1994). Within a sample of young people admitted to secure accommodation in England, over 60 per cent had improved prospects and about one-third markedly improved life chances. Most altered their patterns of relationships and, apart from those with entrenched history of law-breaking, rates of serious reoffending after discharge were low (Bullock, Little and Millham 1998).

Longer-term outcomes are usually not so rosy for those young people without supportive families to return to. Lack of effective follow-up support means that many older adolescents do poorly when they leave residential units, so that gains in self-esteem or behaviour are often not sustained. Many face poverty, hardship, loneliness and hopelessness (Stein and Carey 1986; Biehal *et al.* 1992; Bullock, Little and Millham 1993a; Triseliotis *et al.* 1995).

Residential care has generally lagged behind foster care and adoption in attending to the needs and perspectives of children from minority ethnic backgrounds. Despite the large numbers of studies carried out on residential care in Britain in the 1990s, there is still a dearth of information about the particular needs and experiences of children from ethnic minority backgrounds. It is now commonly recognised that black children face much greater difficulty in handling racism and clarifying their own sense of self if they are bought up in settings and neighbourhoods lacking positive role models. Yet it is still quite common for black children from ethnically mixed inner urban neighbourhoods to be placed in predominantly white areas, at a distance not only from their families but from anyone of similar background (Mehra 1996; Barn, Sinclair and Ferdinand 1998; Berridge and Brodie 1998). This can lead to alienation and 'identity-stripping', as the children lack exposure to positive black images and role models, and are cut off from familiar customs, food and music (Ince 1998). In contrast, black children placed in homes in their own locality with mixed staff groups appear to have a positive identity and good links with their family and community (Barn 1993). Certain local authorities have acknowledged that their residential provision lacks appropriate staffing and knowledge to meet the needs of black children, but Barn, Sinclair and Ferdin (1998) also found 'examples of very good work conducted by black residential staff in children's homes, for example on identity issues' (p.69).

Significant differences have been found in the 'success' rates of different types of residential care. In one study, twice as many placements in residential schools as in residential homes were thought to have led to improvements in behaviour and education (Triseliotis *et al.* 1995). This appeared to be related to carefully planned programmes, shared care with families, personalised education and stable staffing. Grimshaw with Berridge (1994) also found that establishments which combined special education and social care produced positive results in the main.

Several British studies carried out in the mid-1990s converged on the conclusion that the children's homes which helped children more than others were those with clear goals and a cohesive staff group operating to openly shared aims (Sinclair and Gibbs 1998; Brown *et al.* 1998; Whitaker, Archer and Hicks 1998). Bullock (1999) concluded from his review of relevant research that punitive regimes tended to be less successful than more caring establishments. For instance, an evaluation of a long-stay therapeutic community showed that this achieved high levels of satisfaction and subsequent employment for its residents, with its emphasis on individualised education, emotional warmth and close support appearing to be important factors (Department of Health 1998).

Conclusions

This chapter has focused on the current patterns of residential care to be found across most of Western Europe and North America, with particular reference to the situation in the UK. Many commonalities were identified. The numbers of children in residential care are generally much reduced compared with 10–20 years ago; the great majority of the 'children' are in fact young people aged 12 and over. Most stays are short. Whereas in the past residents had a broad spectrum of levels of difficulty, nowadays most have serious developmental or behavioural problems.

Medium-sized residential schools continue to play an important role, but otherwise children's homes have generally become very small – no bigger than a large family. It has become increasingly unusual for staff to spend their working lives in the same establishment and most now live off the premises. Thus homes have become more intimate and personalised, but also characterised by frequent changes of both child and adult occupants. British research evidence suggests that residential care in the 1990s does often help young people, at least in the short run, but with some exceptions tends not to have a significant impact on long-term prospects.

These developments contrast with patterns in Eastern Europe and parts of the developing world, where many children are growing up in large institutions, often with little prospect of leaving, except to move on to a similar sized establishment catering for older children. Despite some determined efforts to change, economic, social and political factors mean that the situation in many countries continues to resemble that which existed up to 50 or 60 years ago in the West.

A further feature which is said to characterise the present-day children's home in the West is its greater openness compared with its larger predecessors, which were often set apart physically, socially and psychologically from the surrounding community and from children's areas of origin. Current child care principles now emphasise partnership with parents and continuity of experience and identity for children. In the next chapter we shall explore the extent to which such openness really exists with regard to children's family and social networks, and examine more closely the theoretical and empirical basis for inclusiveness.

References

Aarre, K. (1998) 'The child welfare debate in Portugal: a case study of a children's home.' In R. Edgar and A. Russell (eds) *The Anthropology of Welfare*. London: Routledge.

Agathanos-Georgopoulou, H. (1993) 'Greece.' In M. Colton and H. Hellinckx (eds) *Child Care in the EC*. Aldershot: Arena.

Ainsworth, F. (1997) *Family Centred Group Care: Model Building*. Aldershot: Ashgate.

Ainsworth, F. and Fulcher, L. (eds) (1981) *Group Care for Children: Concepts and Issues*. London: Tavistock.

Alderson, P., Brill, S., Chalmers, L., Fuller, R., Hinkley-Smith, P., Macdonald, G., Newman, T., Oakley, A., Roberts, H. and Ward, H. (1996) *What Works?* Ilford: Barkingside.

Arieli, M. (1991) 'Caring for "problem" children in the increasingly open residential setting.' In M. Gottesman (ed) *Residential Child Care: An International Reader*. London: Whiting and Birch.

Bagley, C., Po-Chee, G. and O'Brian, C. (1997) 'Hong Kong.' In M. Colton and M. Williams (eds) *The World of Foster Care*. Aldershot: Arena.

Barn, R. (1993) *Black Children in the Public Care System*. London: BAAF/Batsford.

Barn, R., Sinclair, R. and Ferdinand, D. (1998) *Acting on Principle: An Examination of Race and Ethnicity in Social Services Provision for Children and Families*. London: BAAF.

Barth, R.P. (1992) 'Child welfare services in the United States and Sweden: different assumptions, laws and outcomes.' *Scandinavian Journal of Social Welfare 1*, 36–42.

Beedell, C. (1970) *Residential Life with Children*. London: Routledge & Kegan Paul.

Berridge, D. (1985) *Children's Homes*. Oxford: Blackwell.

Berridge, D. (1994) 'Foster and residential care reassessed: A research perspective.' *Children and Society 8*, 2.

Berridge, D. and Brodie, I. (1996) 'Residential child care in England and Wales: the inquiries and after.' In M. Hill and J. Aldgate (eds) *Child Welfare Services*. London: Jessica Kingsley Publishers.

Berridge, D. and Brodie, I. (1998) *Children's Homes Revisited*. London: Jessica Kingsley Publishers.

Biehal, N., Clayden, J., Stein, M. and Wade, J. (1992) *Moving On*. London National Children's Bureau.

Brennan, O.D. (1994) 'Ireland: Changes and new trends in extrafamilial care over two decades.' In M. Gottesman (ed) *Recent Changes and New Trends in Extrafamilial Care*. London: Whiting and Birch.

Brown, E., Bullock, R., Hobson, C. and Little, M. (1998) *Making Residential Care Work: Structure and Culture in Children's Homes*. Aldershot: Ashgate.

Bullock, R. (1999) 'Residential care.' In M. Hill (ed) *Effective Ways of Working with Children and their Families*. London: Jessica Kingsley Publishers.

Bullock, R., Little, M. and Millham, S. (1993a) *Going Home*. Aldershot: Dartmouth.

Bullock, R., Little, M. and Millham, S. (1993b) *Residential Care: A Review of the Research*. London: HMSO.

Bullock, R., Little, M. and Millham, S. (1998) *Secure Treatment Outcomes*. Aldershot: Ashgate.

Charles, G. and Gabor, P. (1988) *Issues in Child and Youth Care Practice in Alberta*. Lethbridge: University of Lethbridge.

Cliffe, D. with Berridge, D. (1992) *Closing Children's Homes: An End to Residential Care?* London: National Children's Home.

Colla-Muller, H. (1993) 'Germany.' In M. Colton and W. Hellinckx (eds) *Child Care in the EC*. Aldershot: Arena.

Colton, M. and Hellinckx, W. (eds) (1993) *Child Care in the EC*. Aldershot: Arena.

Cseres, J. (1994) 'Hungary: Current trends and new perspectives in youth care.' In M. Gottesman (ed) *Recent Changes and New Trends in Extrafamilial Care*. London: Whiting and Birch.

Department of Health (1998) *Caring for Children Away from Home*. Chichester: Wiley.

Dickens, J. and Watts, J. (1996) 'Developing alternatives to residential care in Romania.' *Adoption and Fostering 20*, 3, 8–13.

Dinnage, R. and Pringle, M.K. (1967) *Residential Child Care: Facts and Fallacies*. London: Longman.

Downs, S.W., Costin, L.B. and McFadden, E.J. (1996) *Child Welfare and Family Services*. White Plains, New York State: Longman.

Frommann, A. and Trede, W. (1994) 'Trends in youth welfare work in Germany.' In M. Gottesman (ed) *Recent Changes and New Trends in Extrafamilial Care*. London: Whiting and Birch.

Gibbs, I. and Sinclair, I. (1998) 'Private and local authority children's homes.' *Journal of Adolescence 21*, 5.

Gilligan, R. (1993) 'Ireland.' In M. Colton and W. Hellinckx (eds) *Child Care in the EC*. Aldershot: Arena.

Gooch, D. (1996) 'Home and away: The residential care, education and control of children in historical and political context.' *Child and Family Social Work 1*, 19–32.

Grimshaw, R. with Berridge, D. (1994) *Educating Disruptive Children*. London: National Children's Bureau.

Heywood, J.S. (1978) *Children in Care*. London: Routledge & Kegan Paul.

Hill, M., Murray, K. and Rankin, J. (1991) 'The early history of Scottish child welfare.' *Children and Society 5*, 2, 182–195.

Hill, M., Triseliotis, J., Borland, M. and Lambert, L. (1996) 'Outcomes of social work intervention with young people.' In M. Hill and J. Aldgate (eds) *Child Welfare Services*. London: Jessica Kingsley Publishers.

Hogan, D. (1998) 'The psychological development and welfare of children of opiate and cocaine users: Review and research needs.' *Journal of Child Psychology and Psychiatry 39*, 5, 609–620.

Holman, B. (1996) *The Corporate Parent: Manchester Children's Department 1948–1971*. London: NISW.

House of Commons Health Committee (1998) *Children Looked After by Local Authorities*. London: The Stationery Office.

Ince, L. (1998) *Making it Alone*. London: BAAF.

Kadushin, A. and Martin, J. (1988) *Child Welfare Services*. New York: Macmillan.

Kahan, B. (1994) *Growing up in Groups*. London: HMSO.

Kelly, G. and Pinkerton, J. (1996) 'The Children (Northern Ireland) Order 1995: Prospects for progress?' In M. Hill and J. Aldgate (eds) *Child Welfare Services*. London: Jessica Kingsley Publishers.

Kemppainen, M. (1994) 'Trends in Finnish Child Welfare.' In M. Gottesman (ed) *Recent Changes and New Trends in Extrafamilial Child Care*. London: Whiting and Birch.

Kent, R. (1998) *Safeguarding Children*. Edinburgh: The Scottish Office.

Levy, A. and Kahan, B. (1991) *The Pindown Experience*. Stafford: Staffordshire Council.

Levy, Z. (1994) 'The care process in a residential community setting.' In M. Gottesman (ed) *Recent Changes and New Trends in Extrafamilial Care*. London: Whiting and Birch.

Lindsey, D. (1994) *The Welfare of Children*. Oxford: Oxford University Press.

Madge, N. (1994) *Children and Residential Care in Europe*. London: NCB.

Marshall, K., Jamieson, C. and Finlayson, A. (1999) *Edinburgh's Children*. Edinburgh: The Scottish Office.

Mehra, H. (1996) 'Residential care for ethnic minorities children.' In K.N. Dwivedi and V.P. Varma (eds) *Meeting the Needs of Ethnic Minority Children*. London: Jessica Kingsley Publishers.

Melhbye, J. (1993) 'Denmark.' In M. Colton and W. Hellinckx (eds) *Child Care in the EC*. Aldershot: Arena.

Millham, S., Bullock, R., Hosie, K. and Haak, M. (1986) *Lost in Care: The Problem of Maintaining Links Between Children in Care and their Families*. Aldershot: Gower.

Packman, J. and Hall, C. (1998) *From Care to Accommodation*. London: The Stationery Office.

Parker, R. (1988) 'Residential care for children.' In I. Sinclair (ed) *The Research Reviewed*. London: HMSO.

Plasvig, K. (1991) 'Denmark.' In M. Gottesman (ed) *Residential Child Care: An International Reader*. London: Whiting and Birch.

Poso, T. (1991) 'Welfare for girls, justice for boys? Treatment of troublesome youth in the Finnish residential child welfare system.' In A. Snare (ed) *Youth, Crime and Justice*. Oslo: Norwegian University Press.

Poso, T. (1996) 'Family as framework: Gendered residential treatment of troublesome youth.' *International Journal of Child and Family Welfare 1*, 1, 70–81.

Pringle, K. (1998) *Children and Social Welfare in Europe*. Buckingham: Open University Press.

Quinton, D. and Rutter, M. (1988) *Parenting Breakdown*. Aldershot: Avebury.

Rowe, J., Hundleby, M. and Garnett, L. (1989) *Child Care Now: A Survey of Placement Patterns*. London: BAA.

Rutter, M. (1981) *Maternal Deprivation Reassessed*. Harmondsworth: Penguin.

Scottish Office (1998) *Services for Children 1996*. Statistical Bulletin. Edinburgh: Scottish Office.

Sellick, C. (1998) 'The use of institutional care for children across Europe.' *European Journal of Social Work 1*, 3, 301–310.

Sellick, C. and Thoburn, J. (1996) *What Works in Family Placement*. Ilford: Barnardos.

Sinclair, I. and Gibbs, I. (1998) *Children's Homes: A Study in Diversity*. Chichester: Wiley.

Skinner, A. (1992) *Another Kind of Home*. Edinburgh: Scottish Office.

Stein, M. and Carey, K. (1986) *Leaving Care*. Oxford: Blackwell.

Tam, T. and Ho, M. (1993) *Shared Parenting: Residential Child Care in Hong Kong*. Hong Kong: University of Hong Kong.

Tisdall, K. (1996) 'From the Social Work (Scotland) Act 1968 to the Children (Scotland) Act 1995: Pressures for change.' In M. Hill and J. Aldgate (eds) *Child Welfare Services*. London: Jessica Kingsley Publishers.

Tizard, B. (1977) *Adoption: A Second Chance*. London: Open Books.

Trapp, H-J. and von Wolffersdorff, C. (1991) 'Astride the frontiers between education and punishment: Youth services and juvenile justice in West Germany.' In M. Hill (ed) *Social Work and the European Community*. London: Jessica Kingsley Publishers.

Triseliotis, J., Borland, M., Hill, M. and Lambert, L. (1995) *Teenagers and the Social Work Services*. London: HMSO.

Triseliotis, J. and Russell, J. (1984) *Hard to Place*. London: Heinemann/Gower.

Triseliotis, J., Sellick, C. and Short, R. (1995) *Foster Care*. London: Batsford.

UNICEF (1997) *Children at Risk in Central and Eastern Europe*. Florence: UNICEF.

Vaaben, L. (1994) 'Denmark: perspectives on child care: the nineties.' In M. Gottesman (ed) *Recent Changes and New Trends in Extrafamilial Care.* London: Whiting and Birch.

Van den Bergh, P.M. (1994) 'The care process in a residential child care institutions.' In M. Gottesman (ed) *Recent Changes and New Trends in Extrafamilial Care.* London: Whiting and Birch.

Van der Ploeg, J.D. (1993) 'The Netherlands.' In M. Colton and W. Hellinckx (eds) *Child Care in the EC.* Adlershot: Arena.

Vecchiato, T. (1993) 'Italy.' In M. Colton and W. Hellinckx (eds) *Child Care in the EC.* Aldershot: Arena.

Waldfogel, J. (1998) *The Future of Child Protection.* Cambridge, Massachusetts: Harvard University Press.

Walgrave, L., Berx, E., Poels, V. and Vettenburg, N. (1998) 'Belgium.' In J. Mehlbye and L. Walgrave (eds) *Confronting Youth in Europe.* Copenhagen: AKF.

Whitaker, D., Archer, L. and Hicks, L. (1998) *Working in Children's Homes: Challenges and Complexities.* Chichester: Wiley.

Zamfir, C. and Zamfir, E. (1994) *The Situation of the Child and Family in Romania.* Bucharest: UNICEF Romania.

CHAPTER 2

Inclusiveness in Residential Child Care

Malcolm Hill

Introduction

Significant changes in child welfare philosophies have occurred in recent decades, affecting ideas about foster family care and adoption, as well as residential care. One particular aspect has been a re-evaluation of the role of birth families, particularly in relation to children who experience long-term separations. It has become increasingly recognised that it is neither possible nor desirable in most circumstances to close the door on a child's past and make a completely fresh start. Usually attachments and loyalties have been established. Families have struggled to care for their children, often in very adverse circumstances. With assistance and the passage of time, they will usually be in a position to resume care or at least offer support again. Even when serious rejection or abuse has occurred, relatives can have a continuing role in helping children with their sense of identity and understanding of the realities of their past. For these and other reasons, policy and practice favours inclusive forms of foster care, whereby parents and other relatives are encouraged to remain involved. Even when children are legally and permanently transferred from one family to another through adoption, it is no longer expected that the child's awareness of his or her origins should be minimised (Triseliotis 1973). The shift to 'open adoption' means that some kind of ongoing contact continues between adoptive and birth families, although face-to-face meetings remain rare (Fratter 1996; Hill and Shaw 1998).

For some time now, residential care has been urged to be more inclusive of birth families, to become what Ainsworth (1997) has termed 'family-centred'. However, practice has often remained primarily focused inwards on the children and activities of the unit. Early texts on the tasks and practice of residential care barely mentioned children's families (e.g. Beedell 1970). Even some more recent works make little reference to children's family links or to the role of the residential worker in promoting contacts and helping the child with family and peer relationships (e.g. Kahan 1994). The curriculum of the North American child and youth care education programmes have only a small component about family work (Ainsworth 1997). In this chapter, we shall examine first the evidence about the involvement of parents and others in children's establishments, then review the place of family and network relationships within theories and models of residential child care.

First we examine levels of contact, then staff activities in relation to families.

Contact

Let us consider first what we mean by contact. Given the normal intimacy of family relationships, face-to-face contact is evidently a usual expectation, but telephone calls, letters and perhaps soon the Internet provide other means of maintaining communication in addition to or instead of personal meetings. When there has been a long gap, Masson, Harrison and Pavlovic (1997) suggest it can be useful to begin with telephone contact or to exchange photos and videos, to help children and their parents get reacquainted.

Family members may meet their children in the family home, the children's home or in another setting such as social work office or school. As in relation to divorce, taking children on outings may avoid awkwardness and help the occasion to be a pleasurable one. Third parties like care staff or social workers may be present – to assist the process, assess the relationship or offer protection for the child (Cleaver 1997). Links involve contacts with significant places as well as people. They can involve taking and keeping objects, presents or mementoes (Millham *et al.* 1986).

The precise arrangements will vary according to the circumstances, taking account of the age of the child, quality of family relationships and practical considerations, such as distance or the availability of suitable rooms. Even in favourable circumstances 'managing a visit, either as a guest or a host, is a complex interaction' (Millham *et al.* 1986, p.99). The family relationships of children in care are in addition often marked by tension, conflict or strong emotions.

Attention has mainly focused on parental contact, which in practice for many children means contact with mothers. Yet often other relationships are important, for instance with grandparents, aunts and uncles. When relationships with adult kin are poor, then siblings can be especially important (see Kosonen, Chapter 9). It is also important not to forget children's relationships with friends and others in their previous networks, which may be ignored as professionals focus on the family (see Hudson, Chapter 10).

The purposes of contact may or may not be clear. In the first place, a distinction should be made between parent–staff and parent–child contact (Davidson 1995). These differ in their nature, purposes and implications. Communication between parents and staff usually concerns information exchange, advice, planning, decision-making and, in some instances, treatment.

Overall, the aim of family contact for children is usually to sustain the sense of family belonging and mutual interest, but on particular occasions a host of functions become possible. These include building or rebuilding a stock of shared activities and memories, improving parenting skills, information exchange, providing opportunities for children to voice concerns, reflecting on the past and joint 'work' on problems. Deeper communication often occurs best through and alongside mundane and recreational activities. It is important to be clear whether the interaction is oriented towards the past, present or future, and whether the aim is family reunification or a more independent kind of relationship (Bullock, Little and Millham 1993a; Masson, Harrison and Pavlovic 1997).

The complexity of the tasks means that care staff have a number of options in how they approach contacts. Their roles may include welcomer, facilitator, supporter, counsellor or change-agent, while at times the most helpful thing may be to leave participants alone to develop their relationship as they wish.

Fairhurst (1996) proposed that it is helpful to see parental involvement in terms of phases, with workers taking an active role as 'treatment agents' particularly in the early stages:

- *Engagement.* Staff assess strengths and weaknesses, promote contact.
- *Participation.* Staff seek to change 'child management', for example by modelling different ways of relating to the child; they also maximise opportunities for families to have fun together.
- *Empowerment.* The parents resume charge of the child, e.g. shopping, haircuts.
- *Discharge.* Staff deal with parents' anxieties and remaining problematic behaviour, and offer support.
- *After care.* Continued support.

Initial assessment includes understanding the extent of parental readiness or resistance to cooperation. Negotiation should occur to help the family decide what level of involvement and type of service they are prepared to engage with.

Smit and Knorth (1997) similarly identify stages of staff activity in relation to family contact:

1. *Pre-placement and intake phase.* Visits, sharing of information, clarifying expectations, developing a plan.

2. *Treatment phase.* Contacts; routines; training; support. The homes can send regular bulletins and have phone contacts.

3. *Community reintegration and after-care.*

Drawing on Dutch experience, they stress the particular importance of providing assistance in the final stage to help reintegration. British research, too, indicates that returning home is often a difficult process, as expectations may be excessive, many problems not really resolved and the child's niche at home displaced. Short visits over weekends can give a false 'honeymoon' impression, very different from how things will be when the child is back full-time. Return home revives thoughts and feelings about the original separation and the reasons for it. Views about who was responsible and how well the situation was handled will colour attitudes to the reunion (Farmer and Parker 1991; Bullock, Little and Millham 1993a). Many children in residential care have stepfamily relationships and not uncommonly household composition alters while the child is away (Department of Health and Social Security 1985). Consequently, particular thought is needed to handling the implications of these non-biological family relationships (see Stevens, Chapter 8).

Having considered some of the important issues about contact, let us review evidence about what happens in practice.

The frequency and nature of contact

Research carried out over a number of years has indicated that many children in residential care see their families infrequently, with often negative consequences. During the 1960s and 70s, first in the United States and slightly later in the UK, growing concern was expressed about 'drift' experienced by children in care (Maas and Engler 1959; Rowe and Lambert 1973). It was revealed that many children were placed in residential and foster care without a clear plan or timescale for either reunification with their families or a suitable permanent alternative. One aspect of this poverty in planning was that the children's relationships with their families were often allowed to wither on the vine. On the whole, visits were not actively discouraged but equally no special efforts were made to include parents and other significant relatives, so that only the most dedicated managed to stay in touch.

A series of studies, particularly those using a longitudinal approach, documented what was happening. American research by Fanshel and Shinn (1978) identified in their sample a pattern of increasing isolation for many, with the result that over half had no contact by the time children had been in care for five years, whilst for others visiting was very infrequent. This almost certainly exaggerated the tenuousness of contact overall since the study focused on children in long-stay placements in mainly private agencies. Children in short-term care usually retained closer links with their families. Nevertheless, this study rightly prompted concern about why so many children had become almost de facto orphans, even though their parents were alive and generally also well.

A similar pattern was documented in Britain by Millham *et al.* (1986) who followed up a large cohort of children over a period of two years. By six months the children who were still in care had polarised between those with frequent contact and those with little or none. Over the two years, most children experienced diminution of contact, though for a few the opposite was true. The researchers concluded that three-quarters of children in care experienced some difficulty in maintaining links with their families. For most children, their main contact was with their mother. Where this happened, then contact with other family members was often good too. Fathers were marginal or non-existent in many children's lives. Recent work suggests that more attention should be paid to relatives other than parents since they can provide important support to young people (Marsh 1998/99).

More recent research specifically devoted to residential care has provided a more favourable picture. This may be partly because children in long-term foster care are more likely to have lost touch with their birth families. Also the greater preponderance of adolescents in residential care today, compared both with the past and with foster care, means that relationship and contact issues are different. Whereas younger children are reliant on their parents to keep in touch, older children can take the initiative themselves. However, probably real changes have occurred with social workers, carers and others, now promoting contact more than formerly.

Among the residents of ten children's homes investigated by Berridge and Brodie (1998), half had contact weekly or more frequently. Fewer than one in ten had no family contact. Most staff were positive about maintaining contacts with birth families, but parental visits to units were infrequent. Relationships with parents seemed better than in a similar study carried out a decade previously (Berridge 1985). A similar pattern was found among over a hundred children and young people in the study by Sinclair and Gibbs (1998), except that rather more (one-fifth) had no family contact. Fewer girls had frequent contacts, partly because sexual abuse was sometimes an issue. Sibling contact was also often frequent.

It remains true that those who have stayed in care longer have less contact on average than those in care for under six months. Also, contact is more common for children admitted because of their own behaviour than for those whose admission was related to family stress (Millham *et al.* 1986; Bilson and Barker 1995).

Comparisons with foster care indicate that higher frequencies of parental contact occur for children in residential care (Aldgate 1980). Bilson and Barker (1995) found that the proportions of young people with at least monthly contact were larger in residential care, even when age and reasons for care were allowed for. More of the contact from residential placements is by the child going home, whereas in foster care contact at home or in placement is roughly equal (Bilson and Barker 1995).

Although the majority of parents visit the establishment at least once, most do so only occasionally, relying instead on home visits by their children (Millham *et al.* 1986; Sinclair and Gibbs 1998). Many of the children have 'split-site families', so visits are made to their mother and father living in separate places (Sinclair and Gibbs 1998).

In ordinary children's homes, residents often have considerable freedom to go home whenever they want; but in residential schools and secure care, contact is more controlled by staff as regards timing and place (Triseliotis *et al.* 1995; Bullock, Little and Millham 1998). Overall levels of contact tend to be similar, however. Frequency of contact seems to be less in private homes, probably because they tend to be located away from residents' home areas, though also their specialist functions mean that residents tend to have particularly intractable problems (Gibbs and Sinclair 1998).

The significance of contact
Several quantitative studies carried out over a considerable time span have reached the same conclusion: children who have frequent contact with parents after admission to residential care are most likely to have favourable outcomes and to return home. This is an important and consistent finding which has justifiably been used alongside evidence of low contact to encourage the maintenance of closer links (e.g. Whittaker and Pecora 1984; Department of Health 1991). Nevertheless, some caution is needed in interpreting the data, since contact may simply be an indicator rather than a

cause of overall family relationships. It is after all only to be expected that children who come from 'less problematic' family backgrounds will tend to have parents who are keen to visit, keen to have them home and have difficulties which are more amenable to speedy alleviation. Conversely, when children have little or no contact and poor outcomes, both these characteristics may reflect more severe and deep-rooted family difficulties. It is not necessarily the case that increasing contact in the latter circumstances would have altered the outcomes – though of course it might have done.

With that proviso, let us examine the evidence. Again, one of the early influential studies was that of Fanshel and Shinn (1978) in the United States. They concluded that children who had lost contact with their families had the poorest results, measured on a range of dimensions including emotional turmoil, educational achievement and self-esteem. Similarly, the British study by Millham et al. 1986 showed that children in residential placements with little contact had more emotional problems and were less likely to return home than those with more contact. That it is the quality as much as the frequency of contact which is important was borne out by a study of children going home from care. The main predictors of successful return home were regular family contacts and a child's sense of belonging to the family (Bullock, Little and Millham 1993a). Sustained social work planning and support were important factors, too. Comparable conclusions were reached by a study of leaving care projects (Biehal et al. 1992). Those young people with good family links and opportunities to explore their family histories did best. American research also indicates that reintegration following an episode in care works best when children have kept positive ties with their social networks in the meantime (Whittaker and Maluccio 1989).

In other countries, similar conclusions have been drawn. Lindemann (1991) reported that Swedish research has shown parental cooperation to be 'extremely important for successful treatment' (p.253). A survey of children in care in Hong Kong likewise found that frequency of parent–child contact was correlated with return home (Tam and Ho 1993).

Besides the correlations between contact and outcome measures, more qualitative data indicates the value of maintaining close links, provided this is handled constructively. The studies carried out by the Dartington research unit over the years have suggested that approaches which involve families and help a young person understand the contribution of their family to current difficulties tend to be beneficial (Department of Health 1998; Bullock 1999). In Malmo intensive work by residential units with families prior to and during admission was found to aid cooperation by both children and parents during their stay (Lindemann 1991). In the very different context of a large Portuguese children's home, Aarre (1998) found that although staff assumed that children's family relationships were no longer important, the children themselves were eager to talk to an outsider about their relatives.

Whilst the current presumption is that most children and young people benefit from family contacts and from returning home, it is worth remembering that this is not true for a minority. Farmer and Parker (1991) revealed that some children are not happy to go back home and some are reabused. Sinclair and Gibbs (1998) emphasise that certain young people do better if protected from too much contact, which would otherwise revive problems (see also Quinton and Rutter 1988). Adolescent boys from 'bad' families may be better able to stop reoffending if kept apart (Minty 1987).

Feedback about contact

Recent studies have asked parents and young people their views about the frequency and nature of contact. Most appear satisfied with both. Sinclair and Gibbs (1998) found that just over half of the young people in their sample said that family contacts were helpful. About one in ten regarded it as unhelpful. Very few wanted more contact with parents than they already had. Triseliotis *et al.* (1995) discovered similar high levels of contentment by both young people and parents with the amount of contact. Both studies revealed that a significant minority of young people had at least one family member they would like to see more often or know more about. For some this related to fathers or siblings they had lost touch with or about whom a family secret existed. In the main young people saw social services as encouraging contact and being helpful about it, but a substantial minority saw the department as unhelpful (Sinclair and Gibbs 1998).

Parents generally report favourable relationships with staff in residential care. Some regard them like friends (Brown *et al.* 1998). In the research by Sinclair and Gibbs (1998) nearly all the parents said they were made welcome. Most felt that contact was encouraged, but a minority at a few homes thought they were not encouraged or given enough information. In a two-stage study, a number of parents reported at the follow-up stage that residential staff had helped act as mediators to bring them closer to their offspring (Triseliotis *et al.* 1995). It was not common to have a formal agreement about the type and frequency of contact; these are now advocated as a means of promoting contact (Burford and Casson 1989), though many parents said they do not want one.

Obstacles to contact

Many reasons have been put forward to explain why parents in particular may be loath to visit their children in residential care. Smit and Knorth (1997) refer to 'bottlenecks' which impede not only contact but also reintegration into the community. Some are practical; some are socio-emotional, reflecting the complex processes of contact described earlier. The influences may be grouped into parent, child, setting and agency factors, though often these interact.

PARENT FACTORS

Some parents do lack interest in their children, but this is rarely the sole or even main reason why they find it hard to visit. Millham *et al.* (1986) concluded from their own study that: 'The decline in contact ... may in part reflect the indifference of some parents but it also reflects their powerlessness to intervene, their lack of role and feelings of guilt and inadequacy' (p.117). Parents who have found it difficult to maintain contact report feeling uncertain how to act without guidance or even permission (Masson, Harrison and Pavlovic 1997).

The phrase 'filial deprivation' was coined by Jenkins and Norman (1972) to depict the mixture of guilt, worthlessness and depression which made it hard for parents to summon the motivation and energy to visit children and be reminded of their own failure to care for them. Social workers and carers may then misinterpret parents' confused feelings of anger and rejection as a lack of interest in their children (Berry 1972; Millham *et al.* 1986). Unless staff are very careful, they may reinforce parents' beliefs that they have little to offer. Family responsibilities, pressures and crises may leave little time and energy to visit the child who is away (Berridge and Brodie 1998).

CHILD FACTORS

Younger children are less able to resist contact directly, though the reminder of their original 'rejection' and the continued separation may lead to a negative reaction which discourages parents or staff. Some young people's disenchantment with their parents may lead them to want little or no contact (Triseliotis *et al.* 1995; Sinclair and Gibbs 1998).

SETTING FACTORS

Smit and Knorth (1997) refer to negative staff attitudes which may deter parents. Some may blame the parents for the children's problems or see them as a nuisance. Conscious or unwitting racism may lead staff to hold and express negative attitudes or unhelpful stereotypes about minority ethnic families (Mehra 1996). Staff may wish to protect the children from what they see as abusive parents. In some units, the preoccupation with working with the group of residents may mean that little attention is given to outside contacts (Bullock *et al.* 1990). In an extreme and hopefully rare case, the 'pindown' scandal in England revealed how a treatment philosophy (behaviour modification) could become distorted to deprive children of basic rights, including outside contacts (Berridge and Brodie 1998).

Even when they have positive attitudes, staff can lack the skills and confidence or time needed to support and encourage contact. They may also underestimate the unease felt by family members, despite being given a warm welcome (Sinclair and Gibbs 1998).

Besides the staff, the physical location and layout of the establishment may inhibit contact. Distance can be a significant obstacle, especially as most parents of children in care can ill afford to travel far. The move to more local units means that distance is less of a problem than it used to be (Sinclair and Gibbs 1998). Care of younger children also makes long journeys difficult to undertake. Some buildings are intimidating, whilst no suitable room may be available for comfortable and private interaction.

AGENCY FACTORS

Sometimes courts or responsible authorities place formal restrictions on contact, though these are much less common than invisible restrictions (Millham *et al.* 1986). These limitations result from:

1. Specific restrictions to protect the child from abuse *or* to help placement stability.

2. Rules governing frequency and timing of contact.

A British study in the 1980s (the heyday of access restrictions in the name of permanency planning) showed that access was terminated in three types of situation (Millham *et al.* 1989):

1. long-term care with little prior parental contact

2. situations where social workers think that contact interferes with long-term plans for the child (especially adoption)

3. very serious abuse (only a small number of mainly young children).

In general, parents resent restrictions and prefer to negotiate arrangements.

Although parents often face considerable tangible and intangible obstacles in maintaining contact when their children are in residential care, nonetheless the barriers are not as great as some experience with foster care (Parker 1988; Hess and Proch 1993). In a comparative study, Aldgate (1980) found that mothers generally saw residential staff as more welcoming than foster carers, more flexible about visiting and more willing to let mother and child spend time alone together.

The importance of friends

This book is primarily about family links, but it is important to remember that children have significant links outside the children's unit and besides their families – in particular, friends of similar age. In one study, young people were found to be largely content about their family contacts, but wished to have more opportunities to spend time with friends (Triseliotis *et al.* 1995). Entry to residential care often severs links with close friends (Sinclair and Gibbs 1998). Young people's friends are sometimes seen by staff as a threat, because of joint involvement with drugs, prostitution, crime, etc. Residential carers experience tensions between protecting and not alienating the young person (Whitaker *et al.* 1998). Consequently, many establishments, especially secure units, tend to be much more restrictive about visits to and by friends than family members (Social Work Services Inspectorate 1996). In contrast, leaving care projects in England were found to be particularly good at helping young people develop more friendships through groups, arranging access to mainstream leisure facilities, drop-in centres and so on (Department of Health 1998).

The role of care staff in family links and family work

Although contact between residents and their families seems to have improved in recent years, there is still scope for improvement. Moreover, the fact that much of the contact takes place outside the establishment means that it occurs without any formal input or guidance, and is often separate from staff–family contacts. Arguably it is valuable for the family to have the freedom to conduct their relationship in their own way. Even so, the fact that often problematic family relationships prompted or underlay admission in the first place means that questions need to be asked about the appropriate role for care staff. It seems clear from the above evidence that an active role is needed by staff to encourage contact between residents and their families, and to avoid or help overcome the various obstacles to contact. However, the role of staff in relation to families need not and probably should not be confined to this. Practice texts and feedback from parents suggest that a number of other tasks are possible and often desirable (see e.g. Kahan 1994; Triseliotis *et al.* 1995; Masson, Harrison and Pavlovic 1997; Ainsworth 1997; Department of Health 1998). These include:

- providing good initial information about the nature and functions of the unit; answering parents' queries
- negotiating clearly about the purpose of the particular placement
- discussing respective roles with regard to daily care, schooling, decision-making
- providing feedback about the child's progress
- offering support to parents and other family members
- helping the child or young person's understanding of family relationships
- working with family members together to resolve conflicts or practical difficulties.

These tasks may be carried out by care staff, by specialists working in or attached to the establishment, or by fieldworkers. Traditionally in Britain many of the functions apart from information sharing have been taken on by field social workers. While some residential staff have been content that this allows them to concentrate on their direct care of the child, others have resented being excluded from family work. Many are uncertain about the respective roles of field social worker and residential carer as regards contact and work with families in their own homes (Whitaker, Archer and Hicks 1998). Biehal *et al.* (1992) observed that leaving care projects tended to do little work on family relationships, assuming that field social workers did this.

In North America it has been more common for family treatment to be offered directly from the establishment. Sometimes this role is carried out by separate specialist therapists, caseworkers or counsellors, though perhaps with care staff assisting (McConkey-Radetski and Slive 1988; Kadushin and Martin 1988). Here we shall mainly review the evidence about the role of carers themselves.

Based on their observations of staff activities in a range of children's homes, Whitaker *et al.* (1998) distinguished five core tasks as follows:

- working with the group
- working with individual young people
- surviving as a staff team
- operating within an agency structure
- working with others in the network.

The fifth task included work with families, though also with other agencies and professionals.

Evidence from several countries indicates that the time and attention given to family and network members is often small, compared with that devoted to the children and administrative tasks. Burford and Casson (1989) summed up their understanding of practice and research by claiming that typically 'care and treatment are focused on changing the resident's perceptions, or on changing his or her ways of coping with the family, while nothing is done with the other family members' (p.17).

Concerned about the neglect of family relationships identified in their earlier research, Bullock *et al.* (1990) examined closely the processes of admission of two individual children to an Observation and Assessment Centre. They saw that before and during the early stages of placement staff spent little time with parents. A number of features were absent which could have promoted continuity and sharing. These included:

- no pre-placement visit
- no written information given to parents
- little discussion of the family's role and of future links
- no mention of the logistics of travel
- little concern for personal mementoes.

Subsequently in case conferences, little attention was given to the views of the child and family, or to the implications for family links of the plans made. It would be unwise to generalise from this limited experience of just one home, but these experienced researchers believed that what they witnessed (or rather did not witness) was quite representative of residential establishments they were familiar with.

In their study of several homes in England, Brown *et al.* (1998) detected little consistency in their approaches to families, both between establishments and among staff in the same place. In all but one home, treatment of parents as regards time, welcome and privacy was very different depending on who happened to be on duty at the time. This not only resulted in discontinuity, but meant that parents could be uncertain what kind of reception they could expect.

According to Sinclair and Gibbs (1998) most heads of homes supported family contact, but this was mainly confined to keeping parents informed and encouraging participation in plans for the young people. Most staff wanted to have more involvement with families, care planning and after-care. However, they were often uneasy about tackling family problems and regarded a number of parents as not open to change. When heads of homes emphasised the importance of family relationships, this was linked to improvements in young people's emotional ties to their families (Gibbs and Sinclair 1999).

Research in other parts of Western Europe also indicates low levels of partnership with parents. Danish studies showed that once a child is in residential care, the focus of work and plans tends to be on the child, not the parents (Melhbye 1993). The analysis of case files in Flanders children's homes revealed that only 20 per cent cases had evidence of intensive family-oriented care (Hellinckx, van der Bruel and van der Borght 1993). A Dutch study in the 1980s suggested that only a minority of children's homes were actively working with families (van der Ploeg 1993). A later investigation by Jansen and Oud, cited in Smit and Knorth (1997), concluded that many centres were not very family-oriented and had low expectations about parental change. Although family circumstances were seen as the main cause of placement in 90 per cent cases, these were a target for action in only 32 per cent. Parents rarely took part in meals or leisure activities at the home and only a minority had direct contact with school during the stay. Smit's own study showed that many parents were informed about plans and decisions only after the event, except for decisions to admit and discharge home.

Promoting contact and working with families

Of course, the picture is not uniform and many homes have developed approaches and programmes which aim to work co-operatively with families. Here we present some illustrations of ways in which family participation has been encouraged.

A survey in New England identified a number of agencies which provided concrete assistance to parents, had explicit goals to encourage their involvement in care and planning and had positive staff attitudes. These were found to have high rates of parent–child contact and good staff–parent relationships (Ainsworth 1997). An example of such an agency is described by Villotti (1995). The Nashua Children's Association in New Hampshire committed itself to a family-centred approach in the early 1990s and had to overcome resistance from staff who were used to focusing on the children. Among the key principles and elements of their approach are:

- placing the family (not the child alone) at the heart of planning and treatment

- working with family strengths and seeking to overcome family difficulties

- viewing families as consumers, entitled to simple explanations of the work aims and activities
- staff taking on flexible roles.

Practical examples include scheduling or rescheduling meetings to suit parents as well as professionals; allowing children flexible home visits; having family members for meals; holding parties for all to attend; encouraging parents to use their skills, for example, cooking, music. Many other residential group homes in the USA encourage family members to stay for extended periods, take part in therapeutic, educational and recreational activities, and confer with staff about any significant decision about their children (Downs, Costin and McFadden 1996).

Colton and Hellinckx (1993) concluded their review of developments in Western Europe by observing that in most countries parents' involvement in decisions has grown, but examples of parental participation in care and treatment are still not common. However, several instances of concerted efforts to engage with families as a whole have been documented. An innovation developed in the Netherlands by some residential homes has been to establish intake teams. These meet with the whole family to plan admissions and agree goals and programmes. The hope is to reduce crisis admissions and to make sure there are clear aims for the placements (Van den Bergh 1994). Some Dutch homes encourage parents to retain responsibility for certain daily care tasks, including shopping and washing for the child (Smit and Knorth 1997). A Finnish home encouraged staff to visit family homes and parents to come to the centre to discuss their children and attend family therapy sessions (Poso 1996). This contrasted with two other establishments where family members were either largely ignored or else seen separately by specialist staff conducting family therapy.

Lasson (1994) describes a Danish home which offers treatment for the whole family, who take part in shared activities or therapeutic sessions several times per week. The admitted child lives there full-time, but is joined by parents and siblings at weekends. Emphasis is placed on challenging and confidence-building activities. Parents are helped with relationship and coping problems.

Delameziere and Vicart (1998) provide details of a Child and Family Unit in Northern France for up to five children who stay on average for about 10 months. Admissions are mostly prompted by child abuse. Two social workers live with the children and give social and educational help to parents, who attend frequently for group and family sessions. The Centre aims to support families by helping them play together, have effective rules and appropriate punishments which are not abusive, and guard against risks of sexual abuse. Parents participate in training sessions which cover legal duties about protection, education and reflections on their own behaviour. They attend all key meetings and receive copies of documents. According to Delameziere and Vicart: 'the Child and Family Unit is a structure for meeting and exchanges, where parents and children can learn and relearn to benefit from a positive outlook, something which the majority of such families have so far lacked' (p.55).

Examples of different ways of encouraging parental involvement are also to be found in the UK. All Scottish secure units include in their written aims working in partnership with parents, who are encouraged to visit and keep in touch by phone. The staff help with transport and arrange overnight accommodation. Parents are encouraged to take part in meals and games (Social Work Services Inspectorate 1996). An action research project carried out with respect to children who had lost contact with their parents included a small number in residential care and showed that it was possible to revive relationships (Masson, Harrison and Pavlovic 1997).

Staff in British homes and schools usually offer good support to parents. Most are seen as approachable and easy to talk to (Triseliotis *et al.* 1995). One of the main advantages of residential schools is that young people divide their time between school and home, giving parents a sense of shared responsibility, illustrated by the following quotation:

> Theresa is away but not separated from us. You get a break during the week, but she is home at week-ends. If we have problems at home, we can phone the school and they take it up with her when she goes back. (Triseliotis *et al.* 1995, p.184)

Significant differences in orientation and diverse mechanisms are apparent in the preceding examples. These reflect different goals and views of the staff–parent relationships, though combinations are possible (Table 2.1).

Table 2.1 Types of staff–parent contact

	Process	Goal	Staff role
1	Parents made welcome	Continuity of relationships	Facilitator
2	Parents make contributions to care of the child	Continuity of relationships and empowerment of parents	Partner
3	Parents take part in planning and review	Clear joint planning	Co-decision maker
4	Staff listen and offer guidance	Tension relief	Supporter
5	Staff set tasks for the whole family	Strengthen family coping and bonding	Enabler
6	Staff provide training sessions, family counselling or therapy	Change attitudes and behaviour	Expert change-agent

The extent to which staff retain control of the interactions is variable. In family treatment and parental training models, parents are expected to learn from the professionals 'who know best'. Even in the more participative approaches, parental autonomy tends to remain restricted, with power and responsibility granted or prescribed to parents, rather than assumed by them in the way they want (Braye and Preston-Shoot 1995). The French home described above espouses the principle of *co-education* whereby staff do not take over the child but share responsibilities with the family. Parents are encouraged to share their goals for their children and to negotiate tasks they retain or resume, such as collecting children from school (Delameziere and Vicart 1998).

A development to be found in a number of countries is outreach. Residential units offer help to families in their own home as part of a range of services both on the premises and in the community (Lindemann 1991; Gilligan 1993). This means that not only are a wider range of families assisted, but the same family may receive continuity of service from prevention to in-care to after-care. However, in Britain so far outreach does not appear to have become a fully integrated option, but tends to be offered on an ad hoc basis, depending on the availability of staff and competing demands. Nevertheless, feedback from parents and young people has been broadly positive (Triseliotis *et al.* 1995; Kendrick 1995).

Theories and models of residential child care

Having looked at evidence about current practice, we now briefly review the place of children's families within theoretical frameworks applied to residential child care. This leads on to a review of the rationale for making the child's family more central than has been the case hitherto.

Bullock, Little and Millham (1993b) stated that little theory has been developed about residential child care, in Britain at any rate. Nevertheless, a number of theoretical approaches to residential child care are apparent in the literature or in particular models which have been applied in particular agencies or establishments. These have taken three main forms, each with a number of variants:

1. Focusing on the home, centre or unit.

2. Taking the perspective of the individual child or young person.

3. Considering the place and role of residential homes within the wider child care system or indeed welfare system.

Ideally, of course, a combination of all three is required. Thus, Brown and Clough (1989) refer to the interaction between the individual, group systemic processes and wider structures.

Home-centred approaches

This represents the majority of the literature, though is the least relevant to the main concerns of this book, just because it tends to be inward-looking and focuses on the resident or staff–resident group and its immediate setting. The primary assumption is that the children's experiences with staff and peers will modify their understandings and or behaviour in ways which will enable them to function more effectively when they leave, often to return to their family and home neighbourhood. The latter are seen as a relatively fixed context, beyond the remit of the unit to alter, and to which the child should be helped to adapt. A key concept has been that of the life-space (Beedell 1970) which, though sounding fully inclusive of the external environment, is largely confined to the internal dynamics of the establishment. It encompasses all the interactions of shared daily living, which provide opportunities to learn and develop understanding of social expectations.

Certain of these perspectives do recognise that of course the residence does not exist in isolation, but external links are seen as something to be 'managed' by staff as a peripheral activity (Harris and Kelly 1992). Indeed, the concept of boundary is often central. While earlier models often stressed the need for institutions to have strong protective boundaries, more recently open boundaries have been valued. This is achieved through building designs and staff practices which encourage access, taking account of families' wishes and expectations (Brown and Clough 1989).

Many specific home-centred theoretical frameworks are available, including behavioural, educational, psychodynamic, mental health and systemic (Whittaker 1981; Anglin 1991). Some tend to emphasise the staff's direct influence on the residents through individual and/or group inter-action. Others see staff as facilitating change through mobilising the strengths of the resident group and defusing its counter-cultural tendencies, as in Guided Group Interaction or the Positive Peer Culture model (Brown and Clough 1989; Vander Ven 1991; see also Hudson, Chapter 10). Within therapeutic communities and homes with similar approaches, the whole staff–resident complex is the focus of intervention. This is a prominent model in Israel, for instance (Levy 1994; Amir and Goshen 1994). Although family work is sometimes undertaken alongside group and individual activity, it is secondary within these frameworks. The principal underpinning concepts tend to derive from theories of individual learning and development, or from group dynamics.

Individual approaches

Theoretical perspectives which focus on the individual child may be encompassed within home approaches, as in the case of cognitive-behavioural treatment of young people with histories of violence or abuse. More general frameworks consider children within a broader temporal or socio-spatial context.

Temporal or longitudinal theories place a child's (and family's) current functioning within a sequence of development along a number of interacting dimensions, such as cognition, health, social relationships and identity (Maier 1987; Parker et al. 1991; Ward 1995). The family is important not only for its current role, but also because of its past influence on children's development and sense of who they are, and its future place in the child's trajectory through the life span.

A key longitudinal concept which has been developed specifically in relation to children in public care is the notion of the *care career*. This represents the sequence of places where a child has lived, together with the associated decisions. In the UK, many care careers are characterised by either single brief placements away from home or a string of different placements, perhaps interposed with returns home. Many young people in longer-term care have experienced both residential and foster care (Rowe, Hundleby and

Garnett 1989; Department of Health 1991). In Eastern Europe, care careers within residential care tend to be more long-term and continuous, with often the only change of residence occurring when a child reaches an age threshold, as between a leagan (nursery) and casa de copii (children's home) in Romania.

Within a career framework, any current residential placement has to be seen as building on and leading to life stages in other settings, including the family but also other alternatives. A child's present needs and functioning derive partly from her or his accumulated history, with experiences of change and separation being particularly significant, and are also related to future possibilities, which usually include return home. Residential staff may take on family support, child protection or after-care tasks to help children and their families before, after or instead of a child's stay in the establishment (see Fariss, Chapter 4). The effectiveness of any particular placement can be judged in terms of its impact on a child's future career. Little, Leitch and Bullock (1995) see that: 'the advantage of this perspective is that it links interventions with choice and behaviour and provides an interactive model. Key moments can be identified when options open and close and important decisions have to be made' (p.667). Bullock, Little and Millham (1998) describe a child's *career route*, which comprises two aspects:

1. life route: decisions taken by the child and family

2. process: decisions taken by professionals, agencies and courts.

Whilst this distinction is helpful for some purposes, many decisions made by professionals and agencies are made with varying degrees of participation by the child and family – indeed, current principles favour such jointness.

Whereas the career concept emphasises continuities and discontinuities across time, *ecological approaches* stress a child's links outwards – beyond the residential home – to social networks and systems. Ecological theory has mostly been applied to residential care in a generalised way, emphasising the interconnectedness of all the different persons in a child's life and suggesting that long-term change is hard to achieve without taking account of resistances and knock-on effects within the wider network (Whittaker and Maluccio 1989; Colton and Hellinckx 1993). According to Delameziere and Vicart (1998), an ecological view entails not blaming parents, even in situations of abuse, but regards the child's difficulties as part of family difficulties. Evidence over a number of decades has suggested that changes achieved within residential care readily dissipate once a child is back among the countervailing influences of family and peers (Bullock, Little and Millham 1993b).

There remains considerable scope for more specific application of academic and practical understandings of the structures, patterns and functions of network relationships (see e.g. Mitchell 1969; Ekeh 1974; Cochran *et al.* 1990; Fuchs 1995). The family normally has a central place within the significant social network, but friends, professionals and others are important too, which in turn reflect past and present environment stresses and influences. Enhancing 'natural support networks' should be a consistent element of intervention from before placement through to after-care support (Pecora *et al.* 1992; Downs, Costin and McFadden 1996).

Family systems ideas have been influential in highlighting the importance of dealing with children's needs through working with the whole family (Anglin 1991; Ridgely, Chapter 6). Burford and Casson (1989) argue that concepts from family systems theories should imbue residential staff training and practice, though without adopting the pathological orientation which characterised much family therapy until more flexible, user-friendly methods were developed in the early 1990s (Reimers and Treacher 1995). Key concepts include persistent interdependence, circular causality and patterned communication predicated on need-meeting behaviour. While family systems theory is inclusive of parents and siblings, it has often tended to leave out wider kin and other members of the social network.

Recently, growing attention has been given to the twin concepts of *resilience* and *vulnerability* (Rutter and Rutter 1993; Fonagy *et al.* 1994; Gilligan 1997). Although related to an individual child, the concept recognises that resilience or vulnerability are the product of both personal and interpersonal characteristics. This can be seen as combining career and network, since resilience refers to the accumulated individual strengths and social supports which enable a child to overcome adversity, whilst vulnerability refers to the opposite, i.e. personal characteristics together with conflictual relationships or social isolation which lead to persisting difficulties. Research suggests that certain individual qualities such as a personal competence, intelligence and a sense of humour contribute to resilience. External factors such as social support and educational opportunities can also be vital in helping a youngster overcome adversity. This highlights the importance of helping a child in residential care to sustain contacts with key support figures in their lives, whether family members, friends, teachers or whoever. When these are lacking, then it becomes critical to seek to furnish the child with at least one adult who can act as a supporter and advocate (Cleaver 1996).

Systemic approaches

Residential child care has been located within a wider set of socio-political relationships in a number of ways. Ainsworth and Fulcher (1981) adumbrated a set of twelve factors which influenced the goals and operations of residential units:

- social policy mandate and focus
- siting and physical design of the centre
- personnel complement
- patterns in the use of time and daily activity
- admission and discharge practices
- social customs and sanctions
- social climate of the centre
- links with family, school and community
- criteria used for reviewing and evaluating performance
- theoretical and ideological determinants
- cost factors in service delivery
- organisational turbulence external to the centre.

This framework (updated by Fulcher 1996) provides a helpful and comprehensive analysis of the main influences on centres and also takes account of variations between countries and cultures, though the individual child and temporal dimensions of the life span and career perspectives are lacking.

Thinking about children's homes has been illuminated by noting commonalities with 'institutions' for adults (Goffman 1968) and with other forms of 'group care' (Ainsworth and Fulcher 1981; Brown and Clough 1989). These have been seen to possess common features regardless of the setting and age of resident, including the tendency to turn inwards and set up barriers towards the outside world, of varying degrees of permeability.

At the same time it is helpful to understand the role of residential establishments within the spectrum of services for children (see Turnbull, Chapter 3). Several writers have noted that residential care serves a number of purposes for the wider child care system, such as providing a safety valve or safety net. Challenging individuals are removed to residential establishments to make it easier for foster care or home-based services to operate successfully (Berridge 1985; Parker 1988). Indeed, closed or secure institutions perform a similar role for mainstream residential homes (Wolffersdorff, Kersten and

Sprau-Kuhlen 1989; Harris and Timms 1993). These examples highlight the need for service managers and planners to develop the role and functions of particular establishments in relation to the range of provision available, including foster care and day support (see Turnbull, Chapter 3).

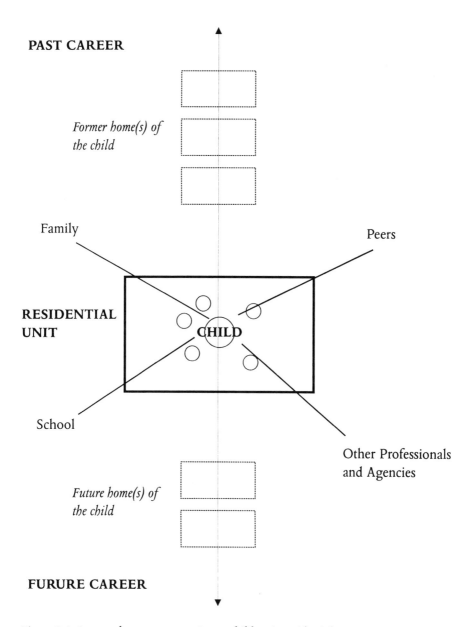

Figure 2.1 A network-career perspective on children in residential care

Broader child care movements and philosophies have had significant implications for residential care. The main thrust of policy and practice over the last two decades in North America and the UK has been to prioritise support to birth families or placement in alternative family settings. Whatever the guiding principle -- normalisation, permanency planning, use of the least restrictive alternative, minimal intervention, continuity -- the emphasis has been on the desirability of family life (Harding 1991; Vander Ven 1991; Fulcher 1996). Hence residential placements have been seen as something to be avoided except as a last resort, despite valiant efforts to highlight that they can and should be a positive choice for some individuals (Wagner Report 1988; Skinner 1992). Britain and North America were most strongly affected by permanency principles, with an emphasis on speedy return home or else seeking permanent alternative families, by use of the law if necessary. In the UK in particular, a further implication of permanency planning was that the continuing role of parents was often marginalised once they were thought to have 'failed' to respond to support to keep the family together (Masson, Harrison and Pvalovic 1997). Countries in continental Europe remained more willing for children to remain in foster or residential care for long periods without considering severance of family ties (Barth 1992; Madge 1994).

The perspectives outlined above may be combined as shown in Figure 2.1 to provide an aide-memoire for the elements residential staff need to understand and take account of in their work.

The rationale for a more inclusive approach to children's families

Ideas about 'the family' have long been prominent in thinking about residential child care. Especially in the nineteenth Century, residential homes were seen as havens, where children were rescued from victimising families. As awareness grew of the often deleterious effects of large institutions, the emphasis changed so that residential homes were now made to resemble families as much as possible. Family group homes were fashionable in Britain from the 1950s to early 1970s, but then gave way to a more 'professional' service. In places like New Zealand, they continue to be important (Fulcher 1996), whilst in certain parts of the world they have been recently introduced as a means of humanising services (Laufer 1996; Bagley, Po-Chee and O'Brian 1997). Re-creations of the family within residential homes have often entailed the notion that birth families can be largely replaced by the substitute setting (Aarre 1998), though in some cases birth family contact has been encouraged (Levy 1994). Reproduction of conventional gender-based roles has also been a common feature of the family group/houseparent model (Poso 1996).

Thus it is possible to identify a spectrum of family–residential home relationships, with three main stances (Davis 1981; Thoburn 1988):

- *Family substitution care.* Acts as a long-term family-like alternative to the original family, e.g. family group home

- *Family alternative care.* Offers something different from family life on a longer-term basis, e.g. therapeutic community

- *Family supplementary care.* Provides respite or focused care with a view to the child returning home soon, e.g. children's unit.

A few rare initiatives have provided 'whole family care', usually for lone parents (see e.g. Gibson and Noble 1991).

Ainsworth (1997) made a simpler distinction in comparing what he called *traditional group child care* (TGCC) with the model he favoured, *family-centred group care* (FCGC). Whereas TGCC substitutes for 'defective' families, FCGC aims to work positively with families. Forms of TGCC often recognise the contribution of families to current problems, but regard the role of residential homes as helping the child overcome deficits and distortions in relationships through insights or social learning in the home, rather than by modifying family interactions (Beedell 1970). Ainsworth suggests that: 'Even today this TGCC model continues to be influential and remains the backbone of many group care facilities' (p.5). Similarly, Little and Kelly noted the all-or-nothing approach of long-stay therapeutic communities: i.e. that either the residence could alone deal with the problems or that for some young people nothing could be done (Department of Health 1998). By contrast, FCGC aims to 'preserve and, whenever possible, to strengthen connections between children in placement and their birth parents and family members' (Ainsworth 1997, p.35). It aims for optimum involvement by the child in family life, even when total reunification is not possible. Implications include:

- offering services, e.g. transport costs and parent education

- involving parents in information-sharing and staff decisions

- openness to parents and others.

Although developments on the ground are patchy, the present trend is to favour family inclusion. Models of residential care which promote family contact and community integration are being applied in Eastern Europe and the Third World (Sellick 1998). We are now in a position to summarise the main factors and rationale for this development.

First, inclusive approaches to the family are seen as in keeping with theoretical perspectives which emphasise the importance for children of continuity and identity in their relationships and the ongoing significance of family and network relationships. These tenets are also reflected in recent policy trends, which in North American terms favour family preservation and restoration (Ainsworth 1997; Berrick, Barth and Gilbert 1997) or in British terms promote partnership and family support (Harding 1991; Aldgate *et al.* 1995). Important concepts informing recent policy, like 'deinstitution-alisation', 'normalisation', 'community-based' and 'least restrictive', all emphasise openness to a child's past and signification network, rather than an inward-looking approach to residential care.

The longstanding debates about the appropriate balance in roles among parents, the state and children was sharpened in the 1980s, when permanency planning fostered a greater use of the law to enable child welfare agencies to override parental wishes when they thought it was in children's interest to do so. This was countered by groups and individuals who advocated on behalf of birth families. These were dubbed 'kinship defenders' by Harding (1991). They emphasised the strengths and positive contributions of birth families. Ainsworth (1997) saw family-centred group care as closely aligned to kinship defenders in philosophy. This perspective recognised that poverty and environmental stresses characterise most families of children in residential care, so that the role of the state should be to alleviate external pressures and provide family support, rather than denigrate and exclude birth relatives. According to Delameziere and Vicart (1998), a key principle is that even abusing parents retain *citizenship*. Their rights to a continuing relationship with their children should only be overridden in extreme circumstances. They need help in overcoming stigma and shame. Moreover, parents are experts on their children and have detailed information and understandings to contribute, as well as emotional and practical support (Smit and Knorth 1997).

The permanence movement gave more credence to overriding parents' interests and wishes in the interests of children where necessary. Also in some ways it devalued the contribution of residential care. Even so, it emphasised that – at least within a Western context – residential placements should not aim to be a family substitute. Instead, residential facilities were encouraged to 'view treatment services as temporary interventions that must incorporate elements of a child's home and community life' (Jenson and Whittaker 1987, p.83; Gibson and Noble 1991).

Second, inclusiveness has legal support. Principles of continuing parental responsibility and of separated children's rights to maintain family relationships (unless it is clearly contrary to their best interests) are included in the UN Convention on the Rights of the Child and increasingly in national legislation. In England and Wales, Section 34 of the Children Act 1989 states that local authorities shall allow reasonable contact between a looked after child and his or her parents. The part of the guidance to the Act which deals with residential care affirms that in the majority of cases personal meetings between children and their parents are desirable (Bilson and Barker 1995). The Children's Home Regulations state that there should be space in residential homes for family and friends to visit; also a telephone where young people can make and receive private calls (Willow 1996). Moreover, parents now have rights of appeal against formal restrictions on access (Millham *et al.* 1989). A duty to promote family contact so long as this is consistent with the child's welfare is also present in Scottish legislation (Tisdall 1997).

Similarly, in France parents retain their rights and duties with respect to children in residential care, except insofar as they are specifically curtailed by a legal order (Delameziere and Vicart 1998). The emphasis of Finnish and Swedish legislation is on supporting parents in their role. Access may be denied only when contact would otherwise endanger the safety or development of the child (Kemppainen 1991; Barth 1992). Dutch law requires parents to be involved in the choice of residential placement. There must be a treatment plan whose development and review should normally involve parents (Smit and Knorth 1997). In Denmark child care law encourages precise planning with details of the purpose of stay away from home and of the support to be offered to the family (Vaaben 1994).

Third, many elements of the research evidence reviewed earlier also support inclusive approaches. Studies of attachment, separation and identity showed the continuing significance to children's development and self-esteem of family relationships, even when these are interrupted and problematic (Maier 1987; Ainsworth 1997). Most children in care retain strong family loyalties (Smit and Knorth 1997). A key argument in favour of family-centred approaches in the USA has been the knowledge that parental contact is a strong indicator of later success and most children will return to their families anyway (Villotti 1995).

Evidence about what happens to children and young people following residential care has been influential. This has shown that for the great majority their existing social network, and most often relatives, continue to be very important as carers or supporters (Biehal *et al.* 1992; Bullock, Little and Millham 1993a). This can include siblings, grandparents and 'honorary kin' (Marsh 1998/99). Moreover, change achieved by children within residential care is hard to sustain, unless supportive improvements have also occurred in the home environment (Jenson and Whittaker 1987; Bullock, Little and Millham 1993b; Berrick, Barth and Gilbert 1998). This means that return home should be treated as a major transition which needs to be carefully managed by residential staff and others to optimise preparation, continuity and support (Farmer 1993).

Implementing inclusive approaches

Adopting an inclusive approach can be interpreted in many different ways, as the earlier review of current practice revealed. For instance, Ainsworth (1997) highlights staff's expert or treatment role in 'teaching' parents how to look after their children and to maintain active connections, whereas other approaches towards parents are more joint and enabling. In contrast, Whittaker and Maluccio (1989) argue for a partnership rather than an expert-led approach: 'if the residential treatment centre is to be seen as a temporary support for families in crises, rather than as a substitute for families that have failed, it must engage families as full and equal partners in the helping process' (p.97).

Among the specific methods advocated are the following (Jenson and Whittaker 1987; Ainsworth 1997; Brown et al. 1998):

- shared decision-making and negotiation of expected contacts and roles, perhaps modelled on family group conferences
- family modification programmes (e.g. parental skills training, family therapy)
- group work (ranging from advocacy to educational models)
- parental contributions to child care and recreational activities within the residential life space
- outreach by staff to provide support in the home environment
- practical aid to improve the child's home environment
- building up parents' support networks
- cooperating with and helping develop community services.

Practical assistance (e.g. with transport and overnight accommodation for parents) is required to support these activities. Often active reaching out to parents is necessary to gain their commitment (Kadushin and Martin 1988). With the move to very small homes, it can be difficult to provide some of these services and support from an individual establishment, since they require specialist resources and a minimum size of parents' group. They may need providing on an agency basis.

Perhaps most important is a persistent orientation by staff to inclusion of parents and other significant family members. This needs to be promoted by agency policy and units' stated objectives, with management and front-line staff negotiating a shared approach to both key principles and detailed responses to the circumstances of everyday living (Burford and Casson 1989; Department of Health 1998). Staff need to understand parents' feelings (like guilt and frustration) and seek achievable ways of working with them which can lead to a sense of shared success (Kadushin and Martin 1988; Halliday, Chapter 5). It is important that residential staff have the training, support and role clarity to undertake planned and consistent cooperation with families. Sensitivity to racism and cultural diversity is also essential.

Based on their own detailed observations, Whitaker *et al.* (1998) propose five main elements in this:

- seeking every opportunity to work together with parents
- promoting a young person's capacity to relate well with parents
- supporting contact, for example, by making available in the home suitable space and uninterrupted time
- recognising limitations to partnership
- acting according to careful assessment, not wishful thinking.

Berridge and Brodie (1998) suggest that the respite or 'short breaks' model developed for children with disabilities may have transferable lessons for residential care more generally. They refer to an 'enhanced integrated model', largely based on this approach. Here residential care is part of a long-term plan to assist families, with placements organised on a planned basis, unlike the emergency admissions which are currently typical. Also the service is seen as meeting the needs of all the family members, parents have power over and responsibility for children's daily care and there is frequent liaison with parents. At the same time great efforts are put into making the experience of the child away from home as productive as possible. A further strength is the strong interdisciplinary input, for example, by health and education specialists.

Conclusion

Undoubtedly residential care in much of Western Europe and North America has become more 'family-friendly' over the last few decades. The evidence suggests that contact between children and their parents tends to be encouraged more than in the past and has become more frequent. A number of agencies and projects have introduced new participative ways of relating to children's families. However, progress has been uneven. Many tangible and less visible obstacles to cooperation remain, while some forms of family inclusion act *on* rather than *with* families.

The rationale for promoting more family-centred approaches must take account of parents' rights and responsibilities, and of the pressures and problems they face. However, it must ultimately be based on children's needs and rights – to family belonging, continuity, identity, choice. A cautionary note is required, since for a few children the risks of continued family involvement may be too high, though even then this is likely to apply to only some abusive family members and not all. In addition, small numbers of young people may want minimal family involvement or struggle to live socially acceptable lives unless family and peer relations are strictly controlled (Sinclair and Gibbs 1998).

In the great majority of cases, however, legislation, theory and research favour maximising family inclusion. This chapter has outlined a number of ways in which this can be done. The chapters which follow provide more detailed accounts of how inclusiveness is being tackled in a range of countries and contexts.

References

Aarre, K. (1998) 'The child welfare debate in Portugal: A case study of a children's home.' In R. Edgar and A. Russell (eds) *The Anthropology of Welfare.* London: Routledge.

Ainsworth, F. (1997) *Family Centred Group Care: Model Building.* Aldershot: Ashgate.

Ainsworth, F. and Fulcher, L. (eds) (1981) *Group Care for Children: Concepts and Issues.* London: Tavistock.

Aldgate, J. (1980) 'Identification of factors influencing children's length of stay in care.' In J. Triseliotis (ed) *New Developments in Foster Care and Adoption.* London: Routledge and Kegan Paul.

Aldgate, J., Tunstill, J., McBeath, G. and Ozolins, R. (1995) *Implementing Section 17 of the Children Act – The First 18 Months.* Report to the Department of Health, University of Leicester.

Amir, E. and Goshen, Z. (1994) 'Residential education: The integrative approach.' In M. Gottesman (ed) *Recent Changes and New Trends in Extrafamilial Care*. London: Whiting and Birch.

Anglin, J.P. (1991) 'Canada.' In M. Gottesman (ed) *Residential Child Care: An International Reader*. London: Whiting and Birch.

Bagley, C., Po-chee, G. and O'Brian, C. (1997) 'Hong Kong.' In M. Colton and M. Williams (eds) *The World of Foster Care*. Aldershot: Arena.

Barth, R.P. (1992) 'Child welfare services in the United States and Sweden: Different assumptions, laws and outcomes.' *Scandinavian Journal of Social Welfare 1*, 36–42.

Beedell, C. (1970) *Residential Life with Children*. London: Routledge & Kegan Paul.

Berrick, J.D., Barth, R.P. and Gilbert, N. (eds) (1997) *Child Welfare Research*. New York: Columbia University Press.

Berridge, D. (1985) *Children's Homes*. Oxford: Blackwell.

Berridge, D. and Brodie, I. (1998) *Children's Homes Revisited*. London: Jessica Kingsley Publishers.

Berry, J. (1972) *Social Work with Children*. London: Routledge and Kegan Paul.

Biehal, N., Clayden, J., Stein, M. and Wade, J. (1992) *Moving On*. London: National Children's Bureau.

Bilson, A. and Barker, R. (1995) 'Parental contact with children fostered and in residential care after the Children Act 1989.' *British Journal of Social Work 25*, 367–381.

Braye, S. and Preston-Shoot, M. (1995) *Empowering Practice in Social Care*. Buckingham: Open University Press.

Brown, A. and Clough, R. (eds) (1989) *Groups and Groupings*. London: Tavistock/ Routledge.

Brown, E., Bullock, R., Hobson, C. and Little, M. (1998) *Making Residential Care Work: Structure and Culture in Children's Homes*. Aldershot: Ashgate.

Bullock, R. (1999) 'Residential Care.' In M. Hill (ed) *Effective Ways of Working with Children and their Families*. London: Jessica Kingsley Publishers.

Bullock, R., Hosie, K., Little, M. and Millham, S. (1990) 'The problems of managing the family contacts of children in residential care.' *British Journal of Social Work 20*, 591–610.

Bullock, R., Little, M. and Millham, S. (1993a) *Going Home*. Aldershot: Dartmouth.

Bullock, R., Little, M. and Millham, S. (1993b) *Residential Care: A Review of the Research*. London: HMSO.

Bullock, R., Little, M. and Millham, S. (1998) *Secure Treatment Outcomes*. Aldershot: Ashgate.

Burford, G. and Casson, S.F. (1989) 'Including families in residential work: Educational and agency tasks.' *British Journal of Social Work 19*, 19–37.

Cleaver, H. (1996) *Focus on Teenagers*. London: Department of Health.

Cleaver, H. (1997) 'Contact: The social workers' experience.' *Adoption and Fostering 21*, 4, 34–40.

Cochran, M., Larner, D., Riley, D. Gunnarson, L. and Henderson, C.R. (1990) *Extending Families: The Social Networks of Parents and their Children*. Cambridge: Cambridge University Press.

Colton, M. and Hellinckx, W. (eds) (1993) *Child Care in the EC*. Aldershot: Arena.

Davidson, A.J. (1995) *Residential Care*. Aldershot: Arena.

Davis, A. (1981) *The Residential Solution*. London: Tavistock.

Delameziere, G. and Vicart, J-N. (1998) 'Returning children home from placement: How can birth parents be truly involved?' In BAAF *Exchanging Visions*. London: BAAF.

Department of Health (1991) *Patterns and Outcomes in Child Placement*. London: HMSO.

Department of Health (1998) *Caring for Children Away from Home*. Chichester: Wiley.

Department of Health and Social Security (1985) *Social Work Decisions in Child Care*. London: HMSO.

Downs, S.W., Costin, L.B. and McFadden, E.J. (1996) *Child Welfare and Family Services*. London: White Plains.

Ekeh, P.H. (1974) *Social Exchange Theory*. London: Heinemann.

Fairhurst, S.K. (1996) 'Promoting change in families: Treatment matching in residential treatment centers.' *Residential Treatment for Children and Youth 14*, 2, 21–32.

Fanshel, D. and Shinn, E.B. (1978) *Children in Foster Care: A Longitudinal Investigation*. New York: Columbia University Press.

Farmer, E. (1993) 'Going home – what makes reunification work?' In P. Marsh and J. Triseliotis (eds) *Prevention and Reunification in Child Care*. London: Batsford.

Farmer, E. and Parker, R. (1991) *Trials and Tribulations*. London: HMSO.

Fonagy, P., Steele, M., Steele, H., Higgitt, A. and Target, M. (1994) 'The theory and practice of resilience.' *Journal of Child Psychology and Psychiatry 35*, 2, 231–257.

Fratter, J. (1996) *Adoption with Contact*. London: BAAF.

Fuchs, D. (1995) 'Preserving and strengthening families and protecting children: Social Network Intervention.' In J. Hudson and B. Galaway (eds) *Child Welfare in Canada*. Toronto: Thompson.

Fulcher, L. (1996) 'The Old and New Worlds.' In *Proceedings of the International Conference on Residential Child Care*. Glasgow: University of Strathclyde.

Gibbs, I. and Sinclair, I. (1998) 'Private and local authority children's homes.' *Journal of Adolescence 21*, 5.

Gibbs, I. and Sinclair, I. (1999) 'Treatment and treatment outcomes in children's homes.' *Child and Family Social Work 4*, 1–8.

Gibson, D. and Noble, D.N. (1991) 'Permanency planning: Residential services for families.' *Child Welfare 70*, 3, 371–382.

Gilligan, R. (1993) 'Ireland.' In M. Colton and W. Hellinckx (eds) *Child Care in the EC*. Aldershot: Arena.

Gilligan, R. (1997) 'Beyond permanence? The importance of resilience in child placement practice and planning.' *Adoption and Fostering 20*, 1, 12–20.

Goffman, E. (1968) *Asylums*. Harmondsworth: Penguin.

Harding, L.F. (1991) *Perspectives in Child Care Policy*. London: Longman.

Harris, R. and Timms, N. (1993) *Secure Accommodation in Child Care: Between Hospital and Prison or Thereabouts*. London: Routledge.

Harris, J. and Kelly, D. (1992) *Management Skills in Social Care*. Aldershot, Ashgate.

Hellinckx, W., van der Bruel, B. and van der Borght, C. (1993) 'Belgium and Luxembourg.' In M. Colton and W. Hellinckx (eds) *Child Care in the EC*. Aldershot: Arena.

Hess, P. and Proch, K. (1993) *Contact: Managing Visits to Children Looked After Away From Home*. London: BAAF.

Hill, M. and Shaw, M. (eds) (1998) *Signposts in Adoption*. London: BAAF.

Jenkins, S. and Norman, E. (1972) *Filial Deprivation and Foster Care*. New York: Columbia University Press.

Jenson, J.M. and Whittaker, J.K. (1987) 'Parental involvement in children's residential treatment: From pre-placement to aftercare.' *Children and Youth Services Review 9*, 81–100.

Kadushin, A. and Martin, J. (1988) *Child Welfare Services*. New York: Macmillan.

Kahan, B. (1994) *Growing up in Groups*. London: HMSO.

Kemppainen, M. (1991) 'Finland.' In M. Gottesman (ed) *Residential Child Care: An International Reader*. London: Whiting and Birch.

Kendrick, A. (1995) *Residential Care in the Integration of Child Care Services*. Edinburgh: Scottish Office Central Research Unit.

Lasson, S.M. 1994) 'Family treatment in residential homes: The Udby Family Treatment Centre in Denmark.' In M. Gottesman (ed) *Recent Changes and New Trends in Extrafamilial Care*. London: Whiting and Birch.

Laufer, Z. (1996) 'The Family Group Home Cluster.' *Community Alternatives 8*, 1, 43–52.

Levy, Z. (1994) 'The care process in a residential community setting.' In M. Gottesman (ed) *Recent Changes and New Trends in Extrafamilial Care.* London: Whiting and Birch.

Lindemann, J. (1991) 'Sweden.' In M. Gottesman (ed) *Residential Child Care: An International Reader.* London: Whiting and Birch.

Little, M., Leitch, H. and Bullock, R. (1995) 'The care careers of long-stay children: the contribution of new theoretical approaches.' *Children and Youth Services Review* 17, 5/6, 665–690.

Maas, H. and Engler, R.E. (1959) *Children in Need of Parents.* New York: Columbia University Press.

McConkey-Radetski, N. and Slive, A. (1988) 'Family focused treatment services.' In G. Charles and P. Gabor (eds) *Issues in Child and Youth Care Practice in Alberta.* Lethbridge: Lethbridge Community College.

Madge, N. (1994) *Children and Residential Care in Europe.* London: NCB.

Maier, H.W. (1987) *Developmental Group Care of Children and Youth.* New York: Haworth Press.

Marsh, P. (1998/99) 'Leaving care and extended families.' *Adoption and Fostering 22,* 4, 4–14.

Masson, J., Harrison, C. and Pavlovic, A. (1997) *Working with Children and Lost Parents.* York: Joseph Rowntree Foundation.

Melhbye, J. (1993) 'Denmark.' In M. Colton and W. Hellinckx (eds) *Child Care in the EC.* Aldershot: Arena.

Mehra, H. (1996) 'Residential care for ethnic minorities children.' In K.N. Dwivedi and V.P. Varma (eds) *Meeting the Needs of Ethnic Minority Children.* London: Jessica Kingsley Publishers.

Millham, S., Bullock, R., Hosie, K. and Haak, M. (1986) *Lost in Care: The Problem of Maintaining Links Between Children in Care and their Families.* Aldershot: Gower.

Millham, S., Bullock, R., Hosie, K. and Little, M. (1989) *Access Disputes in Child Care.* Aldershot: Gower.

Minty, B. (1987) *Child Care and Adult Crime.* Manchester: Manchester University Press.

Mitchell, J.C. (1969) *Social Networks in Urban Situations.* Manchester: Manchester University Press.

Parker, R. (1988) 'Residential care for children.' In I. Sinclair (ed) *The Research Reviewed.* London: HMSO.

Parker, R., Ward, H., Jackson, S., Aldgate, J. and Wedge, P. (1991) *Assessing Outcomes in Child Care.* London: HMSO.

Pecora, P., Whittaker, J., Maluccio, A., Barth, R. and Plotnik, R. (1992) *The Child Welfare Challenge.* New York: Walter de Gruyter,

Poso, T. (1996) 'Family as framework: Gendered residential treatment of troublesome youth.' *International Journal of Child and Family Welfare 1*, 1, 70–81.

Quinton, D. and Rutter, M. (1988) *Parenting Breakdown.* Aldershot: Avebury.

Reimers, S. and Treacher, A. (1995) *Introducing User-Friendly Family Therapy.* London: Routledge.

Rowe, J. and Lambert, L. (1973) *Children Who Wait.* London: ABAA.

Rowe, J., Hundleby, M. and Garnett, L. (1989) *Child Care Now: A Survey of Placement Patterns.* London: BAAF.

Rutter, M. and Rutter, M. (1993) *Developing Minds.* Harmondsworth: Penguin.

Sellick, C. (1998) 'The use of institutional care for children across Europe.' *European Journal of Social Work 1*, 3, 301–310.

Sinclair, I. and Gibbs, I. (1998) *Children's Homes: A Study in Diversity.* Chichester: Wiley.

Skinner, A. (1992) *Another Kind of Home.* Edinburgh: Scottish Office HMSO.

Smit, M. and Knorth, E.J. (1997) 'Parental involvement in residential care: Fact or fiction?' In W. Hellinckx, M. Colton and M. Williams (eds) *International Perspectives on Family Support.* Aldershot: Arena.

Social Work Services Inspectorate (1996) *A Secure Remedy.* Edinburgh: SWSI.

Tam, T. and Ho, M. (1993) *Shared Parenting: Residential Child Care in Hong Kong.* Hong Kong: University of Hong Kong.

Thoburn, J. (1988) *Child Placement: Principles and Practice.* Aldershot: Gower.

Tisdall, E.K.M. (1997) *The Children (Scotland) Act 1995 – Developing Law and Practice for Scotland's Children.* Edinburgh: The Stationery Office.

Triseliotis, J. (1973) *In Search of Origins.* London: Routledge and Kegan Paul.

Triseliotis, J., Borland, M., Hill, M. and Lambert, L. (1995) *Teenagers and the Social Work Services.* London: HMSO.

Vaaben, L. (1994) 'Denmark: Perspectives on child care: The nineties.' In M. Gottesman (ed) *Recent Changes and New Trends in Extrafamilial Care.* London: Whiting and Birch.

Van den Bergh, P.M. (1994) 'The care process in residential child care institutions.' In M. Gottesman (ed) *Recent Changes and New Trends in Extrafamilial Care.* London: Whiting and Birch.

Van der Ploeg, J.D. (1993) 'The Netherlands.' In M. Colton and W. Hellinckx (eds) *Child Care in the EC.* Aldershot: Arena.

Vander Ven, K. (1991) 'United States.' In M. Gottesman (ed) *Residential Child Care: An International Reader.* London: Whiting and Birch.

Villotti, D. (1995) 'Embracing the chaos: Moving from child-centred to family-centred.' *Residential Treatment for Children and Youth 13*, 2, 41–52.

Wagner Report (1988) *Residential Care: A Positive Choice.* London: NISW.

Ward, H. (1995) *Looking After Children: Research into Practice.* London: HMSO.

Whitaker, D., Archer, L. and Hicks, L. (1998) *Working in Children's Homes: Challenges and Complexities.* Chichester: Wiley.

Whittaker, J.K. (1981) 'Major approaches to residential treatment.' In F. Ainsworth and L. Fulcher (eds) *Group Care for Children.* London: Tavistock.

Whittaker, J.K. and Pecora, P. (1984) 'A research agenda for residential care.' In T. Philpot (ed) *Group Care Practice.* London: Community Care.

Whittaker, J. and Maluccio, A.N. (1989) 'Changing paradigms of residential services for disturbed and disturbing children: Retrospect and prospect.' In R.P. Hawkins and J. Breiling (eds) *Therapeutic Foster Care.* Washington DC: Child Welfare League of America.

Willow, C. (1996) *Children's Rights and Participation in Residential Child Care.* London: National Children's Bureau.

Wolffersdorff, C., Kersten, J. and Sprau-Kuhlen, V. (1989) 'Closed units in institutions for children.' In J. Hudson and B. Galaway (eds) *The State as Parent.* Dordrecht: Kluwer.

CHAPTER 3

Meeting Children's Needs Through Integrated Practice in Perth and Kinross

Andrew Turnbull

Over the past ten years there have been great changes in ways of delivering services to vulnerable children and their families. In Perth and Kinross this has meant fundamental changes to the roles of staff, and in particular to the roles of residential staff. More importantly, the changes which are being made have proved more effective in meeting individual needs of children and young people. In this chapter I aim to:

- help the reader to understand the changes, and the reasons for making them
- show how these changes have improved the opportunity to meet assessed needs positively
- demonstrate that new legislation in the form of the Children (Scotland) Act 1995 will add momentum to the progress made within Perth and Kinross Council in providing an integrated approach to delivering services to children, young people and their families.

The context

In Scotland local authorities, known as councils, are still major providers of services to children and families, principally through the Departments of Education and Social Work. Health services, which are also major providers, are funded by central government and work closely with councils to ensure that a broad range of mainstream provisions are made available. The voluntary and private sector work in partnership with the council in many areas of work, and services are commissioned from them.

As regards social work, this means that casework, family placement, community resource and mainstream residential services are all provided by councils, with services being commissioned from the voluntary and private sector where needs dictate. For example, more specialist residential care provision with education may be purchased from the voluntary or private sector.

This model of service delivery provides councils with opportunities, and responsibilities, to deliver a comprehensive and coordinated approach to meeting needs of children and families within the council area, in partnership with other relevant service providers.

Council policies are, of course, rooted in Scots law, and up until 1997 the principal statute in regard to social work practice was the Social Work (Scotland) Act 1968. The creation of Children's Hearings as an alternative to court was a key element of the 1968 Act, and in quite a radical way it moved the approach in working with children and families from a confrontational model to a model which concentrated on the welfare of the child, with courts only intervening in extreme cases. This model and the welfare principles of the 1968 Act have been crucial to policy development in Scotland for nearly thirty years.

Such has been the success of the Children's Hearing system that it has survived the transition to new legislation in the form of the Children (Scotland) Act 1995 which was fully implemented in April 1997. Although the role of courts has greater emphasis within this Act, the welfare principle so crucial to the Children's Hearing system is just as important to the 1995 Act since it has, at its roots, the principles of the UN Convention on the Rights of the Child.

The other important factor to mention about the Children (Scotland) Act 1995 is that it is not an Education Act, or a Social Work Act, but a Children Act which recognises rights of children and responsibilities of parents and councils in partnership with other relevant agencies. It consequently underlines the duty of councils to promote the welfare of vulnerable children through effective use of resources which are available to them.

This chapter concentrates principally on integrated approaches to meeting children's needs from a social work perspective, though the opportunity through the new Act for councils to produce a strategy for a coordinated or integrated approach to service delivery on a wider basis is mentioned later.

Background to developments – policy and research

Perth and Kinross is a geographically diverse area of some 5311 square kilometres, much of which is rural. The city of Perth has a population of 41,000 with the total population of the area being over 130,000, 32,000 of these being in the 0–18 age range. It is also relevant for the reader to know that until April 1996, Perth and Kinross was not a unitary authority, but part of the former Tayside Regional Council which took in the city of Dundee, as well as the new Angus Council area. Policies mentioned consequently make reference to Tayside Regional Council, as well as the new Perth and Kinross Council.

As one of the two rural councils which joined with Dundee City to form Tayside Region, Perth and Kinross in the mid-1980s had a surplus of residential homes which provided accommodation for children and young people, many of whom were from outwith the area, principally Dundee.

In 1987, Tayside Regional Council, concerned at the high proportion of children and young people entering residential care and moving away from their own homes and communities, published a key document which set out principles based on research done, on which the development of new services should be made. The document, *Children in Crisis* (Bates 1987), accurately reflected the position of many children who were in the residential care system. This became policy, with the conclusions and recommendations including:

- There needed to be an integrated strategy which was not currently evident
- Too high a proportion of young people were in care or under supervision
- A clearer value base was required
- Greater emphasis needed to be put on community assessment and support
- Alternative family care should be promoted and developed
- Residential care should be used only where it was identified as meeting assessed needs
- Effective work with other agencies must develop and improve.

Two further studies underlined the difficulties. First, Jeni Vernon, in a study published in 1995 called *En Route to Secure Accommodation* commissioned by Tayside Regional Council, found that all twenty-five young people who had been placed in secure accommodation over the period of the study had passed through one or more children's homes *en route* to secure units.

Second, a comprehensive review of the functioning of the 154 homes and schools which are run by, or registered with, local authority social work departments was carried out by the Chief Inspector of Social Work Services in Scotland in 1992. The report, entitled *Another Kind of Home*, confirms that 'the most significant link between all forms of residential care in this country is that ... they share roots either in the Poor Law of 1834 or in reaction to it ... Institutions providing residential care necessarily involved reactions to perceived social problems, rather than to the expressed needs or rights of individuals.'

Most of the oral and written evidence submitted to the review indicated widespread concern at the poor quality of care experienced by young people and children. Young people felt degraded, staff seemed unsure of their purpose and too many young people did not know what the plans were for them. Parents felt powerless. Education provision was inadequate for most young people.

There were, however, examples of good practice, care and devotion and the report concluded that residential care is not a residual service, or the last resort when all else fails, but it has positive roles to play. The question the report left with councils was how to enable residential care to play these roles well, and how to ensure that residential care could become part of a continuum of social work service delivery alongside other social work community services. Despite the many positive recommendations relating to improving structure, rights of children, lessening stigma, promoting inter-agency planning, and staff training and conditions, this report did not come to firm conclusions about when residential care was a positive choice, and when it was not. Without this guidance, major efforts by councils could be wasted trying to fix systems which are not inherently fixable.

As a former residential worker, and taking on new responsibilities in the late 1980s for line managing the children's residential units in Perth and Kinross, I found that *Children in Crisis* put into context the potential dangers of residential care, and how, if it were to be a positive force, it would require a radical change in approach. For, although units had become stage by stage smaller since I first worked in one in the early 1970s, the outcomes for young people had clearly not improved. That this is still the case is illustrated in a English study *When Leaving Home is also Leaving Care* (Social Services Inspectorate 1997) which, among other findings, demonstrates that 75 per cent of care leavers have no academic qualifications of any kind, and 38 per cent of young prisoners have been in care.

Effects on children and young people

The position for children and young people in Perth and Kinross in 1989 was much as that described in the reports. Although three large homes of over sixteen beds had closed in the late 1980s, not all of which were used by Perth and Kinross children, over 1.4 children per thousand (0–17) were in residential care with the majority of these being placed outwith their home and community.

In Perth, with the recent closure of two large units, there remained three units: of eight beds, four beds and two beds. Despite being small in relation to units I had worked with in Strathclyde Region, the two larger units exhibited the same difficulties for young people. They were entering residential care, usually on an emergency basis in the midst of a family crisis. At this most vulnerable time, where skilled and sensitive intervention was vital to gain their confidence, children and young people were frequently confronted, despite the best efforts of the staff, with an environment of confusion. They not only saw wide differences in age range, but more importantly they began to live in an environment with other young people with different sets of needs. It did not take long for young people to learn that they could control the situation through negative behaviours. Issues of power and control being constantly tested led to a potentially unsafe environment for young people and staff, as well as having a detrimental effect on community relations due to the lack of commitment to the unit felt by the young people. In these situations staff would resort to an autocratic management style, leaving young people feeling excluded or frustrated.

As line manager, I was more than aware through night-time calls, and unit and community meetings, that needs of young people were not adequately being met in this environment. The initial problems which needed to be addressed with young people and their families were being exacerbated by the turmoil of group living. Individuals would, within a day or two, find ways of surviving within the group which often mitigated against the ability of staff to work with them. Deterioration in behaviour often led to a change in care plan, and possibly a change in unit. A high percentage of young people moved on to a residential school or secure unit where this had not been envisaged at the time of admission.

While much emphasis was rightly put in reports such as *Another Kind of Home* (Skinner 1992) on staff training, and clear functions and objectives, the ability of councils to control admissions to the extent that the individual's needs matched the resource was very limited. Children and staff were being wrongly blamed either for their behaviour, in the case of the children, or their inability to manage, in the case of staff. In Perth and Kinross the management team recognised that a new, more individually based approach was required if we were not to continue to make situations worse for children and young people. While the voluntary and private provider could gatekeep in order to have a group which could live and work together effectively, a new approach was needed to meet the needs of young people entering the care system for the first time. It is fortunate that, council policies encouraged us to move down a non-traditional route. Not only were needs not being met but budgets were being stretched to breaking point by the number of inappropriate placements in residential schools. Surely these resources could be better spent by meeting individual need in a different way!

The move to integrated practice

Organisational change

In the late 1980s, the approach was still very much service-led. The different components of all child care services were separately managed. Fieldwork, residential care, intermediate treatment and family placement were all managed within different structures, by different managers, in different geographical locations (sometimes twenty-five miles away from Perth). Assessing and meeting needs was therefore a rather haphazard process which could not reach satisfactory levels of consistency. Staff were confused about understanding and accessing services, so for consumers the process must have been a mystery.

The first helpful step was taken by Tayside Region in 1989 where a divisional, decentralised model took away the functional splits between residential, fieldwork and community services and placed them together under one manager. This structure gave the opportunity to follow the recommendations of *Children in Crisis*, deliver a more coordinated service delivery to young people locally, and with it get teams, including residential, to work together on meeting assessed needs of individual children and young people.

Impact on staff

Bringing teams together poses many challenges. Boundaries are threatened – and myths are exposed about what teams do (and do not do) – before progress can be made in recognising each other's skills and potential contributions. At the start the word 'integrated' was not so much on our minds as 'divided'. Residential staff criticised social workers for not visiting, not speaking to them or not valuing their input. Social workers accused residential staff of doing their own thing and paying attention only to bad behaviour. Both accused intermediate treatment workers (now community resource workers) of doing nothing and they in turn accused everybody else of doing the wrong things! Or so it appeared!

As a manager for services for young people over the age of 12 responsible for fieldwork, residential and community resource teams, my first goals established with the senior workers involved were to help teams to be clear about their own roles and remits, and those of other teams. Polarised structures in the past had led staff to have many misconceptions about what other teams did. Training and joint team-building sessions concentrated on these areas. Job shadowing was introduced. Progress was slower in the residential sector because of traditional rota difficulties and crises in units which did not easily allow staff to come together for team building. An additional factor may have been to do with the initial sense of wariness in residential staff regarding change, status and conditions of service. Understanding between the teams did increase, however, helped in particular by one of the teams having within it family placement, independent living and community resource workers.

Integrated approach of team leaders

The most important catalyst for bringing together the work of the teams was, and continues to be, a twice-weekly meeting where the manager meets with all seniors or team leaders. Although reasonably informal it addresses referrals and current problems, and shares responsibility for resolving identified difficulties. From this meeting flexible responses can often be applied to problems identified by using skills of people from different teams. A common understanding of what constitutes priority work and where to target resources started to develop. Because of management presence at this meeting any necessary decision-making and resource allocation can be made without the need to refer it elsewhere, since budgets are devolved to service manager level. Through this approach, and with policy aims influencing our practice objectives, greater success was achieved in helping children and young people remain within their own families, schools and communities.

Table 3.1 gives the numbers of children in residential homes and schools between 1989 and 1996. The figures do not include an increasing number of placements in alternative families, nor do they show what is for me the most significant decrease within secure accommodation. When our residential units were in crisis and our staff overstretched, secure figures rose and then diminished as our units reduced in size. Admissions are now rare and are not the result of failures in ways of providing residential care.

Table 3.1 Children in residential homes and schools			
	Residential homes	**Residential schools**	**Total**
Oct 1989	10	21	31
Oct 1991	9	13	22
Oct 1993	9	5	14
April 1996	6	6	12

Over 2 per 1000 of 0–18-year-olds in Tayside Regional Council (1.4 in Perth and Kinross) in 1989, fewer than 0.5 per 1000 of 0–18-year-olds in Perth and Kinross in residential care in 1996.

Move to resource centre

Although progress in working together, and in maintaining more families safely in the community, was made between 1989 and 1991, the move of all teams, excluding residential at this stage, to the one resource centre in a former children's home in Perth ensured that people could effectively work together. A walk along a corridor could access main grade staff, seniors or manager. (The residential manager is now also based in the resource centre.)

Residential staff developments

In 1991 there was a much-needed residential restructuring which breathed fresh life into a residential scene that was coping with the transition from younger, longer-term residents, to short stay, more 'troublesome' residents. The units were in crisis, as described earlier. The appointment in 1991 of a qualified Senior Residential Resource Worker and eight qualified residential workers enabled the residential teams (20 staff, 3 units and 14 beds) to become equal partners in the development of the service. It did not, in itself, stem the tide of difficulties that the residents, and consequently staff, were experiencing in the form of frequent absconding, self-harm, harm to others and difficult relationships with neighbours, but it did provide the confidence for the residential team to join forces with the other teams to find a way out of the crisis for young people and staff alike.

Development of co-working

While most new referrals are managed by the fieldwork team alone, others, for whom greater input is required, are allocated support from different teams so that a large degree of co-working develops. Through the development of seniors meetings, more imagination began to be used in considering how to meet the needs of young people in difficulties. For example, the young person out of control in the community, with numerous charges, and on the verge of being placed on an unruly certificate by the police, would often previously have gone to a residential assessment bed. In cooperation with the family, time out – often miles away from Perth – can be arranged for that young person with a resource worker. He or she works closely with that individual while work is simultaneously going on with the family and school to try to develop strengths which can prevent recurrence on his or her return. This approach is quite significant in empowering young people and parents, and in avoiding placing a young person into a system where he or she may quickly deteriorate. Resources offered to the Children's Hearing can include an 'Intensive Community Assessment' which allows six weeks of close work involving young person, family and all involved agencies. The Hearing is, after six weeks, in possession of a comprehensive assessment which can be used to guide decision-making in a more informed way than would otherwise be the case.

Networking is the term we use to describe formal ways of managing co-working between teams. For the small number of young people who require the involvement of two or more members of staff, a senior coordinates a meeting with the identified members of different teams and ensures a care plan is in place with responsibilities defined. The social worker meets on a weekly or fortnightly basis thereafter with other relevant staff to monitor and evaluate progress and make minor necessary adjustments. Seniors will attend on a monthly basis or as required.

This system, more than any, has allowed different teams to acknowledge each other's roles, challenge each other positively and focus jointly on meeting the needs of young people and their families using each other's skills and abilities positively. Residential staff, in particular, have grown in confidence over the years by their active involvement in care planning for the young person and their increasing involvement in family support, not solely for children who are in care.

Research into integrated practice

Throughout this time a study called *Residential Care in the Integration of Child Care Services* was being prepared (Kendrick 1995). As suggested by the title, it focused on the role of residential care in three Scottish local authorities in the context of the integration of child care services, during the period from 1989 to 1993. Of the 201 children studied, it was disturbing, though not surprising, that four-fifths of residential admissions were described as emergencies and that they had a total of 412 placements during the study year. Also of interest was that young people rarely moved from residential placements to foster placements.

This report, which influenced us to progress the route towards an integrated approach to meeting needs, came to a number of interesting conclusions, and there were signs that barriers between fieldwork and residential work could be broken down. Perth and Kinross had been subjects of the study and the benefits of an integrated management structure were highlighted in the report together with the fact that it was taking longer to bring residential services into the integrated model than other teams for a variety of reasons. The recommendation of this report gave credibility to the position that our efforts to adopt an integrated approach to delivering services was correct, but that to be truly integrative, 'strategies must embrace practice and policy at both local and national level'.

Impact on residential care
Beyond the crisis
Effective networking, consistent policy of care in the community over a number of years and development of a Strategy for Young People in partnership with the Education Department has, as predicted, reduced the numbers in residential schools substantially. The new Perth and Kinross Council accepted a committee report in 1996 called *Beyond the Crisis* (Bridgeford and Frew 1996) which outlined the progress made through developing this integrated approach. This report:

- confirmed closure of the six-bed unit (which had had no residents within it for over a year)

- established the principle, and gave the go-ahead, to develop from normal housing stock (i.e. not purpose-built) accommodation for up to 12 young people, with the largest unit accommodating up to three young people

- recognised that residential staff time, should it not be required in unit, should be employed to support families and vulnerable children as a family unit in their community, where this was seen to be in the best interests of the child

- formally recognised that an integrated approach to delivering services was being extended to all ages through the opening of a resource centre for children under 12 and their families.

(All managers were by now pursuing models of coordinating their staff and physical resources to provide effective integrated services.)

Outcomes for staff

The outcomes have not been evaluated in any formal way. However, it has become clear that:

- Staff have greater clarity about their role both in relation to their residential role and in relation to their joint work with community social work colleagues
- Staff have greater job satisfaction gained through a young person's needs not being distorted by others at the time of admission, and the consequent ability of staff to actively pursue the goals of the care plan
- Staff have greater opportunity to work with the family as a whole and promote parental responsibility
- Staff welcome the greater sense of responsibility in not having an 'in-house' hierarchy which diminishes the role they play with young people
- Staff do not feel themselves tied to a building
- There is less interruption in the middle of the night for managers!

Outcomes for children and young people

- Accommodation and transport are 'normal', thus reducing institutional stigma
- Young people's views can be more easily taken into account, and where necessary challenged in a safe environment
- Increased choice is available
- Family contact can be more normally and easily managed
- Irrespective of age, alternatives to family care will be available where this is in the child's best interests
- There is less chance of breakdown in placement
- There is more chance to plan well with the young person the next steps
- There is less incentive or desire to abscond
- There are fewer interrupted nights for young people.

Functions and objectives

While it is vital for schools and specialist units to have statements about purpose, residential care provided by councils needs to take account of differing individual needs. As a consequence functions and objectives of all our homes are now uniform, reflecting our commitment to aim to meet assessed needs of children, young people and their families.

Where do we go from here?

The concept of an integrated approach to meeting needs is now well understood in the Social Work Department. Four managers under the Head of Child Care manage a broad range of services, and the planning function is not seen as separate. All policy and staff guidance developments are channelled through five monitoring groups, which comprise a broad range of staff, including planning officers, prior to decisions being made. Team structures have continued to develop and many teams contain within them social workers, resource workers and social care officers. Children's services as a whole have now adopted an integrated approach to service delivery, and this will ensure that the Social Work Department can deploy its resources and meet assessed needs, among all age ranges. This has been an evolutionary process. The progress, though, is apparent as can be seen through the beneficial effects on children's care plans and outcomes.

As a result of the new requirements made in the 1995 Act, a joint planning structure was agreed in Perth and Kinross involving all Council Departments, Health Trust and Health Board and other relevant agencies to produce a children's services plan for 1998. This plan examines local need and considers how to meet these needs within the resources available. The process leading to the plan, and the continuing monitoring and review of the plan, will ensure that the concept of an integrated approach is extended through time to include all providers of services to children. Even in times of diminishing resources, needs of children and young people will have a better chance of being met through good inter-agency cooperation and coordination between service providers. No doubt complications about boundaries and responsibilities will arise, but that will be the new goal regarding more effective integrated practice in Perth and Kinross. It is encouraging that the residential sector, whose role is now clearer, can join in the planning process as a constructive part of the continuum of services which aim to meet the needs of children and families in Perth and Kinross.

References

Bates, P. (1987) *Children in Crisis – Report to Social Work Committee.* Tayside: Tayside Regional Council.

Bridgeford, B. and Frew, B. (1996) *Beyond the Crisis – Report to Social Work Committee.* Perth and Kinross: Perth and Kinross Council.

Kendrick, A. (1995) *Residential Care in the Integration of Child Care Services.* Edinburgh: Scottish Office Central Research Unit/HMSO.

Skinner, A. (1992) *Another Kind of Home – A Review of Residential Child Care.* Edinburgh: Scottish Office HMSO.

Social Services Inspectorate (1997) *When Leaving Home is also Leaving Care.* London: Department of Health.

Vernon, J. (1995) *En Route to Secure Accommodation?* London: National Children's Bureau.

CHAPTER 4

Partners in Parenting:
Safe Reunification

Nova Fariss

Introduction

In the joint fields of child protection and out-of-home, or substitute, care, the term 'reunification' is used to describe the activity of purposefully returning children into the care of the parent or parents. There is some evidence to suggest that of children who come into care, about 90 per cent are reunified with their family for at least some of the time (Atherton in Diamond 1995). Clearly it is an area of work that covers a wide range of individual and family circumstances, and a variety of case strategies, not all of which are purposeful. Nevertheless, it is acknowledged that many children are able to return home when structural and financial issues are addressed, when a violent partner leaves, or when parents begin to utilise services in their community that alleviate and reduce stress.

At the same time, workers in this field are seeking ways to promote change in families where commonly accepted support services have been unable to create a safe environment in which to return children. Increasingly, definitions of reunification which include meaningful reconnection between children and families as well as full-time return home are reflecting the view that practice in this area still needs to retain a focus on the safety of children (Maluccio, Kreiger and Pine 1991; Gelles 1993).

This chapter will describe a programme operating at Mofflyn, a non-government Uniting Church agency in Perth, Western Australia, which is targeted at children and families where issues of safety require an intensive change-focused approach. The outcomes of this work will be examined, as will the practice issues and dilemmas that have arisen over time and helped in developing the programme.

It is perhaps relevant at this point to avoid any definition of family, other than to acknowledge that the situations from which children enter the care system, and to which attempts are made to return them, are many and varied. The only common feature in these family structures would appear to be the presence of at least one biological parent.

Context

Politically Australia operates under a federal system, with a national or Commonwealth government, eight state and territory governments, and many local government councils. In the area of child and family welfare the bulk of responsibility has rested with the states, with each having separate legislation regarding child protection, out-of-home care, juvenile justice and child care. The Commonwealth has responsibility for the broader issues of social security, such as pensions and benefits, child care rebates, and family law concerning guardianship and divorce. It also represents Australia's international responsibilities regarding children. As the main collector of revenue in Australia, the Commonwealth government can influence the activity of the states through tied grants, funding initiatives and joint ministerial and administrative councils.

Unlike in the United Kingdom, no statutory child and family services or powers have been devolved to local government. This particular tier has tended to provide the more generic child care and family support services, although some councils have become involved in youth accommodation programmes funded by the Commonwealth. The implementation of competition policies in all states has seen some local governments become more active participants in state-funded child and family service initiatives.

The provision of services to children and families at risk at the local level has depended on a combination of regionalised offices and services of the state departments, and access to services provided by the non-government sector. These services are increasingly tied to funding agreements with the state departments, which determine their priorities according to identified need, available resources and political emphasis, as described in their strategic goals.

Trends in service demand have significantly influenced policy. In 1991–92, 53, 296 cases of child abuse were reported in Australia, of which 43 per cent were substantiated (Carmichael 1997). The figures represented an annual increase of 7 per cent. At the same time, Bath (1993) identified that Australia had one of lowest placement rates in the world, with Western Australia's rate at 2 per 1000 children. Recent reports from the Australian Institute of Health and Welfare (1997), which collates interstate data, would indicate that the trend in child abuse reporting has continued, and that the child placement rate has increased significantly over the last two years.

These factors, along with a diminishing out-of-home care resource, have led various state governments, including Western Australia, to consider what services can be provided to prevent children entering care, and to support a more planned and intensive approach to reunification. It has also been well established in Australia (O'Sullivan and Woods 1994) that a large proportion of children in care voluntarily seek to reconnect with their own families in their teenage years. Children, families, carers and agencies have identified the need to prepare children and parents for these reconnections, and improve their quality.

Child and family welfare in Western Australia is covered by the 1947 Child Welfare Act, which is under review. It does not provide for supervisory orders, but children can be made wards of the state for limited periods, or until the age of 18 years. Increasingly the adjournment period is being used to provide some supervisory role for the Children's Court while other work is being undertaken. Children with short periods of wardship can have that period extended by the Minister without the matter returning to Court. Many referrals for reunification have come from the need to satisfy the Minister about extension. Important also is the lack of formal policy concerning permanency planning. Consequently, children in care can be subject to several reunification attempts, and no permanent order or guardianship arrangement be made.

The provision of out-of-home care, placement prevention and reunification services to Aboriginal children and their families has been strongly influenced by the application of Aboriginal Child Placement Principles for almost two decades. These Principles are actively applied within each state, and are endorsed at a federal level. The intention has been not only to provide culturally appropriate placements and services, but also to encourage Aboriginal ownership and management of these agencies. The Principles also allow for Aboriginal families to choose services provided by a mainstream or non-specialist service provider. On average, 25 per cent of children in placement are Aboriginal, although they represent less than 4 per cent of the total population. A landmark report on the history and lessons of removing Aboriginal children from their families and communities was released by the Australian Human Rights Commission in 1997. Entitled *Bringing Them Home*, it has become known as the 'Stolen Report', due to the serious impact of this earlier government policy on the Aboriginal people.

The agency and the programme

Mofflyn is a Uniting Church agency with a seventy-five year history in
residential child care. As such, it has been through all the phases and stages
experienced by others in that area of activity, the most significant of which
was a move in the mid-1980s to provide a home-based alternative to
residential care. (In Western Australia 'home-based' means within the child's
own family, not foster care, as it means in other jurisdictions.) Other
programmes have been developed for adults and children with intellectual
disabilities. However, the change from residential services provided the
opportunity to work with families to divert children from admission to care,
and by 1991 had become the agency's most sought-after service. Within that
home-based service itself a significant shift of purpose occurred over time –
from support and maintenance to change and lowering of risk. This shift of
purpose is linked to the increasing complexity of the families requesting or
being referred to the service, and the increasing intensity of the intervention
provided.

Within this context Mofflyn was asked on a case-by-case basis to
undertake reunification work with extremely high-risk families. It became
clear that a service gap existed in Perth in terms of work that emphasised
goals rather than time-frames, and provided support for statutory decision-
making. It was decided to redeploy resources from a general residential
programme and to establish a specialist service with a residential component
to meet this need. At the same time the home-based team was retained, with
its emphasis on placement prevention and strategies involving direct links
with families in the community.

Partners in parenting

Established in 1994, and based largely on the Family Reconnections
programme at Canterbury Social Services in Victoria (described in Jackson
1995), the aim of this programme was to return children to the care of their
parents safely, or to confirm that other care options needed to be pursued for
the children.

The children's unit was staffed on a roster basis with six family resource
workers and a coordinator, whose training background included child care,
early childhood teaching or mothercraft nursing. A senior social worker was
assigned to the unit. After the social worker and programme manager
received training from Canterbury, all staff were provided with six days'
initial training. Training continued as a monthly activity for all staff, and
focused on working with involuntary clients, the needs of parents, adult

learning, the particular needs of young children, attachment, grief and loss, and dealing with personal attitudes and values.

The social worker was assigned to each family referred, who was also allocated a family resource worker from within the unit. This worker would continue their role within the family home once the child moved from the unit to their parents' care. The use of both workers encompassed the roles of case manager, counsellor, support worker and educator.

To access this programme, children were to be aged seven years or younger, with the possible inclusion of older siblings. Targeting this age group was seen to be consistent with research that showed not only that they were at the highest risk of harm, but also that the likelihood of successful reunification is higher. There is also a greater choice of placement options for children of this age not able to return home. All families were referred by Family and Children's Services, the statutory authority, who remained actively involved. An assessment had been made that the parents initially required supervision during all contact with the children, and this work could not be undertaken through the interface of the child's current foster placement and the family home. Parents had to agree to participate in the programme, although it was accepted that their agreement may have been coerced by the circumstances.

The stages of the work were similar to those described by Jackson (1995) and Fein and Staff (1991). Pre-placement assessment and goal-setting was based on: the parents' acceptance of responsibility and motivation for change; levels of risk and signs of safety in the existing relationship between parents and children; strengths and resources in the family system; and the impact on the children of another placement move.

During the three-month residential phase, children lived in the unit, with parents encouraged and assisted to spend increasing amounts of time learning how to meet their children's needs. Other goals related to the family's own needs were addressed through counselling or more practical forms of assistance, such as locating suitable housing. Addressing historical and lifestyle issues that impact on parenting, and enabling children to describe their own stories and feelings, were important aspects of this phase. Links with specialist agencies in the fields of mental health or substance abuse were maintained and built on as part of the work.

If it was agreed that the family situation was safe enough for children to be returned home without constant supervision, the family were then provided with outreach support for a further three months. Support was initially intensive, tapering off as the parents retained their learning and gained more confidence.

The progress of each family was formally reviewed at six-weekly intervals, and included the state department.

Outcomes

In the first year of operation, the programme received 17 family referrals. Five of these were not accepted, and four were referred to the home-based team. Of the other eight families, three proceeded through the programme to reunification, two had children remain in care, and three were awaiting services.

In the second year of operation, ten families were referred to the service. Again four families were passed to the home-based team. Out of the families remaining in the programme, full reunification occurred with two out of five. At the same time a further 32 families were referred direct to the home-based team, with a full reunification rate of 30 per cent.

Based on the number of referrals, the full reunification outcome rate was low, but not outside the outcomes of other similar programmes (Fein and Staff 1991). In the context of Western Australia's relatively low placement rate, it is not surprising that a case outcome of children remaining in care was as common as that of children returning to the care of their parents. The most successful reunification outcomes for the Partners in Parenting residential programme were for single parents with one child.

Evaluation and programme development

At the time that this original information was presented in Glasgow in 1996, a decision had been made to close the residential programme and put the resources into an increased placement prevention and reunification programme using non-residential approaches. Mofflyn and Family and Children's Services staff had learned a lot about reunification from the operation of the unit and the focus it provided. However, a range of managerial and practice issues emerged that prompted a different direction.

First, for the number of families provided with a service, the residential programme was extremely expensive. Comparatively, outreach-only services provided by the home-based team achieved similar or better outcomes at lower cost.

Second, by shifting placement again, the children bore the most personal cost of this style of work. It is most likely that they bear the highest cost in all reunification work, and the added burden of relocation is not always in their interests.

Third, residential programmes run the risk of creating their own institution with either imperceptible barriers forming toward parents, or parents themselves taking on the care they receive rather than passing it on to their children. The need to operate a residential unit and provide care for children can contribute to workers becoming rigid in their practice, rather than adapting to the culture and lifestyle of the family as a whole.

The age-limit for children being referred to the programme was increased to 12 years, consistent with Mofflyn's placement prevention age-group. However, most referrals would be for children under seven years.

But a structural response is only a partial treatment of the issues. In an examination of research findings regarding reunification programmes, Maluccio, Fein and Davis (1994) concluded that some service packages and special programmes demonstrated power to influence reunification and re-entry outcomes. How this power is exerted has not been fully explored. But Mofflyn's experience is that it has much to do with the values being practised, and how practitioners manage the inevitable tensions between family strengths and risks to children, working relationships with the statutory agency, and understanding and mobilising motivation.

During 1997 staff in the programme reassessed practice based on the agency's values of partnership, working cooperatively and proactively with others, and a belief in the capacity of people to change. Important changes were made:

- Reduce the amount of information needed at the time of referral, and begin contact with the family as soon as possible. In that way, the statutory agency could see themselves as a credible partner, and the assessment work of the programme focused on the issues and needs of the family that would guide the work.

- Have the phases of the work – assessment, supervised contact, unsupervised contact, return home with support – driven by achievement of goals rather than time-frames. The changes and needs of the children have remained important indicators as the work progresses.

- Stay with families as they learn from their mistakes. Their difficulties have taken years to influence their parenting. Change will also take time.

Through these changes staff have been able to retain their child-centredness, whilst persevering with very challenging families.

In order to respond flexibly to children and families, staff in the programme have needed to apply a range of therapeutic skills. Brief therapy approaches such as those described by Berg (1994) have formed the basis of training, along with motivational interviewing, crisis theory, child development and narrative therapy, to name a few. Critical to the work is an understanding of family systems, the ability to apply principles of adult learning as parenting skills are developed, and the ability to assess children's needs as well as family risks and strengths.

The changes in outcomes have been measurable. Between July and December of 1997 the programme worked with as many families as for the previous year (28), and had doubled the rate of full reunification outcomes to eight, with a further nine well into the later stages of the work. At least two of those families had previously been unsuccessful, although the improved reconnection between parents and children that occurred from the earlier work was able to be built on. This is consistent with Ainsworth and Maluccio's (1998) view that reunification services should be offered for as long as possible to maintain the reconnection of the child and family.

Expectations and experiences

The various factors that are likely to influence outcomes have been identified by several writers in this field (Maluccio, Krieger and Pine 1991; Allen 1993; Fein and Staff 1991). They include the length of time the child has been in placement and the amount of parental contact during this time, the child's relationship with a caregiver, the lack of opportunities to teach and learn parenting when children are out of home, the tendency of family systems to reform when children are not present, the child's and family's sense of failure, the lack of a sense of crisis for the family, and the nature of relationships in the service system around the child and family.

Overall, Mofflyn's experience is that the degree to which any or several of these factors are present should be considered at the time of referral. In particular the child's placement history and quality of the relationship with his or her caregiver, and the reasons for seeking reunification at this time, are critical considerations. Nevertheless, the presence of the above factors serve more to guide practice than to predict success or failure.

Whilst reformations in the family unit are described as important considerations, little is said in the literature about the presence of new partners. Mofflyn's experience is that this is often a critical factor in influencing outcomes. New partners need to be acknowledged as part of the work, including an assessment of their own strengths and risks. The parent's need for adult relationships is understandable, and the reasons they make choices that pose risks for themselves and their children are complex and powerful.

Corresponding to the length of time a child has been in placement is the age of the child, and, sometimes, the age of the parent. This programme has been particularly successful with very young children of young parents. It confirms the view that planning for reunification should occur when the child is first placed.

The difficulty of providing teaching and learning opportunities whilst the child lives elsewhere has meant that the work may move into the family's own home as soon as possible, even while the child may still be in placement. Family resource workers have proved invaluable in the role of home-based supporter-educator. Not only do they assist parents, but also the task of transporting children provides an opportunity to see and hear clues from the child about developments in the relationship.

Whilst the work may commence with a lack of a sense of crisis, it invariably does not stay that way. The intrusive and intensive nature of contact with the agency, the deeply personal issues addressed, and the process of change itself, will precipitate crises. A partner may leave, a parent may binge-drink, a violent eruption may occur, a child may disclose abuse. These are points to be used for learning and decision-making.

Perhaps the greatest challenge is dealing with the child's and parents' sense of failure. Building self-esteem has been described by Jackson (1995) as an essential component. In our culture we tend to shun rewards such as certificates, star charts, or treats as things for children. Yet they have proved effective tools in this task.

Staying with families while they learn from their mistakes may sound very positive, but raises the question as to what factors determine when it is safe enough or worthwhile to persevere. This is difficult to establish clearly from the literature, but two factors emerge from Mofflyn's experience. First, whether the parent has increased their awareness of the needs of the child, and second, their own motivation to proceed if encouraged to do so. Examples of these are unsolicited inclusion of the child's feelings in discussing the particular event, and reflecting on their achievements in the work so far.

Flexibility and maturity in social work and family care practice, supported by regular formal supervision and training, is a vital component. There is a fine line between moving at the family's and child's pace, 'dancing their dance' on the one hand, and on the other having the service system reflect family patterns and chaos (Kagan and Schlosberg 1989). Up to 30 per cent of the social worker's time is spent managing or working with the service system around the family (Peerless 1995).

A recent feedback report from a father reunified with his three sons covers most of this discussion:

> The worker knows what it is to fall and fail, and not be out.

Conclusion

When this workshop was first presented at Glasgow in 1996, a participant made the observation that some practices could be seen to be punitive. Little did the workshop participants know they became part of the service development for Mofflyn's reunification programme. Punitive practice is never the intention when services are developed for families where abuse or harm has occurred, but is always a risk.

The Mofflyn reunification programme has developed within a context where political emphasis on parent's rights and responsibilities is not necessarily matched by policies and strategies concerning permanency planning. Whilst reporting to the statutory system is an essential part of the work, evidence gathering to serve this context can divert the programme's focus away from providing real services to families. It can also hamper efforts to build satisfying levels of reconnection where full reunification of the family is not possible.

Nevertheless, inter-agency influence of this programme and the literature and research from overseas and other Australian states has increased awareness about earlier and purposeful consideration of reunification goals and strategies for children in care. As the major funder of Mofflyn's reunification services, and the major service-provider partner in each family situation, Family and Children's Services has now clearly articulated its expectations, roles and responsibilities for organisations undertaking this activity.

Mofflyn's experiences confirm much of the literature and research on reunification and family preservation. The service operates in the area of tension between keeping children safe, and facilitating change in families that have been described as unsafe. In practice this means keeping the child's needs as paramount, whilst allowing for some trial and error as parents put in considerable effort to change patterns established over many years.

It is important to engage the family in the change process as quickly as possible. Assessment is a discernible beginning phase, but also carries its own impact on the family, creating opportunities for experience and learning. Staff need to be able to utilise a variety of therapeutic, solution-focused and life-skill development strategies, and be given supervision, training and opportunities for their practice to be visible. Time limits for the phases of the programme are not necessarily helpful, but review and target dates for phases of the work can provide a useful evaluative framework.

Overall, however, the experience has been that practice should reflect positive values towards families and respect their desire to parent their children more effectively. Mofflyn's mission is to work cooperatively and proactively with others to support and enhance the functioning of families, to reduce the risk of harm to children and to improve the quality of life for people with disabilities. Applying the technology of practice knowledge and research to put agency mission principles into practice has had more influence on positive developments in the programme than the technology alone.

References

Ainsworth, F. and Maluccio, A. (1998) 'The policy and practice of family reunification.' *Australian Social Work 51*, 1, 3–7.

Allen, M. (1993) 'Redefining family reunification.' In M. Allen (ed) *Family Services Newsletter*, 5–7. National Resource Centre on Family Based Services.

Australian Institute of Health and Welfare (1997), 1997 Report. Canberra: ACT.

Bath, H. (1993) 'Family Preservation Services – Do they have a Place in Australia.' Paper presented at W.A. Family Preservation Conference.

Berg, I.K. (1994) *Family Based Services: A Solution-Focused Approach.* New York: Norton.

Carmichael, A. (1997) 'Prevention of child abuse in Australia – a nationwide approach.' *Journal of Child Centred Practice 4*, 1, 25–31. ISPCC.

Diamond, S. (1995) *Literature Review.* W.A. Government: W.A. Out of Home, Preventative and Alternative Care (OHPAC) Planning and Co-ordination Committee.

Fein, E. and Staff, I. (1991) 'Implementing reunification services.' *Families in Society: The Journal of Contemporary Human Services*, 335–343. Family Service America.

Gelles, R. (1993) 'Family reunification/family preservation: Are children really being protected?' *Journal of Interpersonal Violence 8*, 4, 557–562.

Jackson, A. (1995) 'The Reconnections and Family Admission Programs: Two Models for family reunification within Australia.' Unpublished paper, prepared for Canterbury Social Services, Melbourne.

Kagan, R. and Schlosberg, S. (1989) *Families in Perpetual Crisis.* New York: Norton.

Maluccio, A., Fein, E. and Davis, I. (1994) 'Family reunification: Research findings, issues, and directions.' In *Child Welfare 73*, 5, 489–504.

Maluccio, A., Kreiger, R. and Pine, B. (1991) 'Preserving families through reunification.' In E. Tracy, D. Haapala, E. Kinney and P. Pecora (eds) *Intensive Family Preservation Services: An Instructional Sourcebook.* Boston: Mandel School of Social Sciences.

O'Sullivan, R. and Woods, K. (1994) *The Roundabout of Care: A Study of Children / Youths Who are Difficult to Maintain in Stable Placements.* Western Australia Government: Family and Children's Services.

Peerless, H. (1995) *Mofflyn Home-Based Services Programme: Research and Evaluation Report.* Perth, Western Australia: Mofflyn.

CHAPTER 5

Parental Responses to a Complementary Model for Residential Care

Denis Halliday

Note: *Sadly Father Halliday died before he was able to develop this chapter fully. It is presented here in slightly amended form to convey key points from his research.*

The importance of what happens to parents in a residential placement

Parents and children who have been involved in out-of-home placements have contributions to offer in furthering an understanding of the processes and effects of such programmes (Maluccio, Fein and Davis 1994, pp.497, 500, 501). The influence of parents is particularly significant for models of care which regard parents and their households as the basis around which services are arranged. Initially conceptualised by Davis (1981) and promoted by Ainsworth and Hansen (1986), the complementary model of residential care envisages such programmes as complementing or supplementing what parents and their households are already providing and will continue to provide, given appropriate support (Child Welfare League of America 1994). While the term 'family-centred' has gained more recent currency, the focus of the complementary model is on the parents themselves as key players in the situation. It is important to obtain feedback on how residential care programmes affect parents. What follows selects some findings of an investigation of participants' perspectives on a residential facility for male adolescents aged between twelve and sixteen, in Sydney, Australia. It is called Boys' Town, and services households in the greater metropolitan area of this city. It has three residential units and an on-campus school, with youths in residence on a weekday basis during school terms.

Research design

The constructivist or naturalistic approach as developed by Lincoln and Guba (1987) provided the researcher with a methodology to tap the views, feelings and perspectives of respondents, drawing on their core experiences and customary patterns of discourse (Erlandson *et al.* 1993). Accordingly, parents, youths and staff who responded to the invitation to participate were interviewed individually in depth with an open-ended style of recursive questioning to draw out views about how the agency affected the parents in offering a residential placement for their sons. For the purposes of this study, 'parents' were taken to include the natural parents, legal guardians such as adopting parents, or significant relatives who act as the key caregiver at this period of a young person's life. Partners of a natural parent who had no biological connection with a young person (e.g. step-parent) were not invited to participate.

A purposive sample of twenty-one parents and ten young people was drawn from clients who had used the service over the last five years. In eight of the cases where young people took part, one or both parents also did so. Interviews took place either at parental homes or at the agency, while additionally, for some of the youths interviews took place in the near vicinity of their homes. Twenty staff from the different service sectors of the agency were also interviewed to obtain their perspectives on how the agency affected parents in its service delivery. The framework of confidentiality and anonymity gave respondents the protection that no one apart from the researcher would be able to identify their particular contribution. Respondents were given the opportunity to review the transcripts of interviews, prior to arranging final consent to the interviews being used in the study. Adult respondents retained a copy of transcripts, while youths read the transcripts. Although parents had the possibility at their own discretion of sharing their transcript with other family members, the youths would only have been able to give a verbal account of their interview to other family members.

The interviews focused on the reactions of parents to the service offered in the context of the difficulties which precipitated placement and of household and wider network relationships. This chapter highlights the interaction between the placement and developments in the family relationships.

Parents' networks and support systems

The identification and promotion of parents' natural networks and support systems with relatives, friends, work contacts and neighbours has been a key feature of the family preservation movement (Tracey *et al.* 1994). It has also catalysed residential care programmes to incorporate this approach too, instead of leaving the parent in limbo while a resource-rich system sets to work on the resited youth. In this study parental accounts brought out that their networks and support systems interact dynamically with the circumstances which led to the young person's separation from home. In a number of cases the stresses which resulted in residential placement were connected to a need for the household and network relationships to regroup.

Even routine encounters with the public and social space of the local area could have become complicated as a result of the family difficulties which precipitated the need for residential care. Social contacts would be reduced to avoid shame or conflict and it was only after the placement began that the parents began to venture out again:

> We didn't go anywhere. There were very few places where we'd go. That's why. Because it would be … you'd take the war zone with you. So you often left places, parties, or you know, that sort of thing … Or we just wouldn't go. It was, sort of, keep it in our own walls … [laughs] spoil someone else's fun.

Parental access to previous natural networks and resources can become impaired. Three of the parents interviewed mentioned that the particular trouble their household was undergoing with an adolescent son made it difficult or embarrassing for them to talk about it or even spend time with relatives, friends and neighbours:

> We did lose a lot of contact with a lot of people … More so, people just didn't want [my son] in their home. My real close friends, they were different. My family didn't care. They sort of came in and upset things, even worse for [my son] and for me. We sort of, we were sort of going backwards when they were around. They were putting a big damper on everything towards us.

The progress of the placement could affect communication with network members:

> Well, I was waiting to see how [our son] was going at [the agency's] school before I actually went to try to make up with my friends, well, one friend in particular. I did not want to brag about it and then him fall apart.

Two male parents spoke of work-sustained injuries that stopped their involvement in their customary work environment where they had built up conversational associations with fellow male employees. They expressed some disorientation about no longer being accessible to that understated, laconic but helpful sharing of stories by men about family matters, as they had either ended up being relocated to an alternative work area with relative strangers, or had to stay at home where there was no one to talk with. They were no longer able to engage in that more physical interplay between their sons and themselves that both their sons and they were used to. They were under stress but had reduced familiar outlets in which to talk.

These cases illustrate how parents' contacts and communication with different parts of their networks were implicated in and affected by the problems which prompted the placement. Often access to support was thereby weakened, even though the need for it was now greater. On the other hand, there was scope for positive developments too. One parent reported a sharp falling away of one sector of her support system in the aftermath of a bereavement, as it proved difficult or awkward for the parent's social set, a couples' network, to deal with the partner's loss or the changed social status of this person. But in the face of her own subsequent social 'death' in which many intimate friends dropped back to being strictly passing acquaintances, she developed her longstanding involvement in a local sports activity into membership of the committee. In addition to the group support, she connected with a member whose experience of loss of her own partner proved far more helpful to her than her encounters with professional counsellors.

Effect of placement upon siblings

When the young person in placement had been the centre of tension at home, the brothers or sisters could welcome the separation. This might allow a realignment of relationships which proved beneficial in the longer run.

One parent said that she was upset at how pleased the younger siblings were when the older son went into the programme. But to her relief, they eventually moved to looking forward to his return on weekends and school holidays as their relationship with him became less troubled.

Another parent initially thought a younger sibling was 'quite a sadistic little thing' because he went around the house whistling as soon as her son went into the programme. However, it turned out that it was a matter of the brother coming 'out of the shadows'. He felt he had the opportunity to get the attention he wanted, once the placement of his brother began. This led to the mother developing a more clearly defined view of her younger son's personality and needs over the period of the placement:

> I'd never really able to get to know [the younger sibling] because [my son] had, right from birth, he had consumed so much time.

The subsequent affectionate exchange of the younger sibling with this mother was very supportive for her. This mother regarded the discovery of this enhanced relationship with him as one of the most significant aspects of the placement for her.

Another mother said that the placement of her son gave her the prospect of sharing her energy and emotional resources with younger siblings who had come to 'exist on the fringes':

> It had been I guess, four, five, maybe six months of just sheer hell. And [our other two children] just really didn't exist. It was – shove food down them, put them in uniform, send them to school, pick them up and that was it.

In summary, often parental engagement around the child who is the centre of the storm in the household is so preoccupying either at crisis pitch or in a slow and insidious build-up that other children in the household are unable to get the attention from parents that they would like. This came out in four parental interviews. In addition, parents may be deprived of the positive feedback about their role that they might be able to receive from these less troubled children. Hence the removal of the 'problem' child can improve family relationships and parental self-esteem. Unless carefully handled, this may make it difficult for the separated child to return without feeling out of place or disrupting the beneficial changes.

The placement as a safe place

The view that the agency was a safe place for their sons came up in seven parental accounts and in two youths' accounts of their parents' views. Their sons had stayed out late at night, engaged in risk-taking activities that could have led to death by misadventure or acting out suicidal tendencies they had been talking about. In some instances, police were phoning or bringing their son home when the parents were in bed at night. Their perception that the agency was a safe temporary place for their son freed them to sleep at night, and to be released from that sense of chronic stress and worrying that did not help their relationship with their son anyway.

Several parents had themselves had harrowing personal or family experiences. They were aware that they had not been able to protect their sons from some exposure to this. This led them to express gratitude that the agency was a safe place for their sons, relative to the environs that their sons were frequenting prior to the placement. Parents also valued the way in which the agency provided challenging activities and leisure opportunities in an organised and safe way.

Parents relieved that staff will discern the best in their adolescent child

Although parents normally wanted the placement to happen, they still very much wanted continued contact and involvement. Often their past contacts with professionals had not provided help on a cooperative basis. Many of the parents had had dealings with social service organisations which tended to exclude themselves and focused on their adolescent child, or else used the professional technical language of pathology in their discourse about them. While the parents are beset with troubles in their own interactions with these adolescent children, there is still connectedness between them. In their appeal for support, they did not like being advised to give up on them or give them up. Two parents, who in their own way were desperate for assistance at the point of referral, still spoke about their 'unconditional love' for their son. Hence they spoke favourably when their feelings and role were recognised by the agency following a complementary model. Conversely they were unhappy when staff were disillusioned with their sons or themselves.

One staff member noticed the positive insights of parents that stemmed from their deep affection for their adolescent sons. In the act of 'forgoing' their role as a parent by handing their adolescent child over to a unit, one parent wondered 'whether anyone else will take time to see what's loveable about them.' This parent was appreciative that there were staff who 'took the time and looked at not only the negative but looked also at the positive and actually got to like my child'. However, this parent was resentful that some staff, at a late stage in the placement, got weary of dealing with this youth's negative behaviour and wanted to have no more dealings with him.

Two sets of parents described how initially their sons had been viewed in a warm and understanding perspective by staff. Later this moved to a more abrupt and clinical point of view, whether as a result of a change in key staff dealing with the youths or a slow agency drift. It had led to the placement being terminated by the agency. At the time of the interviews this still registered as a shock to these parents who spoke about it.

Four parents spoke of how reassuring it was for them that not only did they themselves have staff to confide in but that the attunedness of these staff to rapport with their adolescent children was reciprocated by the youths.

While an agency may promote in general terms an attitude of partnership between households and the agency, this can often end up being co-option of parents by the agency on the agency's terms, under the banner of 'cooperation'. But these parents gave the sense that this link between the staff member and their adolescent son was a sort of extension of the staff members' relationship with them. It was as if the parents were inviting a keyworker agency staff member into personal partnership with them, to see the best in their adolescent child while being aware of the worst, and daring to be accessible to that adolescent child, despite that youth's history of complications in relationships.

Conclusion

This small study has shown the value of taking account of prior relationships in parents' social networks and the household. The placement often gives opportunities to reassess and realign relationships. Parents may need help in overcoming guilt or embarrassment in order to sustain supportive contacts. Siblings may benefit from the concentrated attention they receive while the young person is away from home, though this clearly means that care is needed to ensure that the gains for the young person or sibling are not undermined when the family is reunited. The study also showed that parents of sons at risk valued the security and protection which they believed was given by the placement. At best, staff in the agency were able to establish relationships of respect and trust with parents. Such staff thereby became an accepted part of the parents' supportive network.

Note

Father Denis Halliday is the co-author of D. Halliday and J. Darmody *Partners with Family in Crisis: Parent Responses to a System of Care.*
The book is available from Boys' Town Engadine, 35a Waratah Road, PO Box 99, Engadine NSW 2233.

References

Ainsworth, F. and Hansen, P. (1986) 'Incorporating natural family members into residential programmes for children and youth.' *Australian Child and Family Welfare* *11*, 1, 12–14.

Child Welfare League of America (1994) Minutes from the Values Subcommittee, of the National Advisory Committee on Group Residential Care, 31 October, 1 November, 1994, p.4. Washington: Child Welfare League of America.

Davis, A. (1981) *The Residential Solution: State Alternatives to Family Care.* London: Tavistock.

Erlandson, D., Harris, E., Skipper, B. and Allen, S. (1993) *Doing Naturalistic Inquiry: A Guide to Methods.* Newbury Park: Sage.

Lincoln, S. and Guba, E. (1987) 'But is it rigorous? Trustworthiness and authenticity in naturalistic evaluation.' *Evaluation Studies Review Annual 12*, 425–437.

Maluccio, A., Fein, E. and Davis, I. (1994) 'Family reunification: Research findings, issues and directions.' *Child Welfare 73*, 5, 489–504.

Tracy, E., Whittaker, J., Pugh, A., Kapp, S. and Overstreet, E. (1994) 'Support networks of primary caregivers receiving family preservation services: An exploratory study.' *Family in Society: The Journal of Contemporary Human Services 75*, 8, 481–489.

CHAPTER 6

Residential Treatment:
A Resource for Families

Elizabeth Ridgely and William Carty

The central idea of this chapter is that residential treatment is a resource for families. The children belong to the family, not to the residential programme. This is a significant paradigm shift in Canada, where the first residential treatment units for children were opened thirty years ago with little involvement from the child's family. The idea at that time was that residential treatment, apart from the family, was therapeutic for the child. Long-term residential treatment, often as long as three years or more, was thought to be curative for disturbed children through milieu, group, activity and individual therapies. There were no outcome studies and little contact with families throughout the treatment process. The toxicity of the family was banished and professional nurturance put in its place.

By the 1970s family therapy was becoming a presence, with the voice of Minuchin *et al.* in *Families of the Slums* (1967) questioning the long-term value of treating children without their families. As more professionals became trained in family therapy, they were less convinced about sending the child away, with the accompanying implicit assumption that the professionals were more competent to raise the child than the family. Throughout this period and into the 1980s, most residential treatment units added family work to the treatment of the child. This was based on a child guidance model with the sharing of information between residential staff and family, maintaining a focus on the child.

As the 1980s proceeded into the 1990s the length of stay in residential units decreased significantly. As we approach the year 2000, the issue of treatment in Canada is and will be related to cost of 'the bed'. The good thing about the cost perspective is that the family will increasingly be seen as the major resource for the child with short-term units resourcing the family.

The George Hull Centre for Children and Families has been operating with such a model for the past fifteen years. Collectively, we have learned from Salvador Minuchin (1967, 1974 and 1984) and the faculty of the Philadelphia Child Guidance Clinic, Maurizio Andolfi (1989) and the International Practicums in Rome and the late Carl Whitaker (Napier and Whitaker 1978). There are many authors and teachers in the field of children and families but we looked to these three child-centred family therapists to 'unlearn' us in pathology and to refocus our thinking on the strengths of families, over time with multiple generations and extended kin, friends and neighbours. As we explored the resources of the family, it became clear that the logical place for a residential unit was alongside other resources of the family for the family to access as it needed.

There are four main ideas which accompany our resource model. The first two ideas are related specifically to the programme. The second two have to do with the families.

The programme

1. Residential treatment is a resource for families and as such it belongs to the family. The child belongs to the family and not to the programme. Families decide admission and discharge to the programme.

2. The primary function is to enhance the competence of families; to facilitate connectedness among family members; to strengthen the sense of belonging, which is at its most vulnerable at the time of admission; to build on the strengths of the child through group and individual programming, thorough assessment, education and recreational activities.

Multi-disciplined planning among child care, social work and psychiatry was essential to ensure the centrality of both the family and of the child.

For the child care worker, the work changed subtly but significantly. The task was to help the child manage and thrive in the programme, while simultaneously keeping the family central to him or her.

The major shift for the worker is toward enhancing family relationships, traditions and preferences rather than enhancing the relationship between the child care worker and the child. The child care worker becomes a 'connector' to the family for the child, not a substitute for mother, father, brother or sister. At the same time, the relationship between the child care worker and the child becomes an alliance for progress in programme activities, as well as for ongoing contact with the family.

Context conversation about who does the dishes in your family while doing the dishes in the programme, or what is your mother's favourite supper while preparing the evening meal, are essential to strengthening and respecting the tie to the family. 'What would your brother think about this movie? Let's call him to find out.'

The programme operates on a group format, in that it is structured for the whole group of children and adolescents, and each child and staff member follows the format on a day-to-day basis. The structures and routines are geared at healthy, normalised expectations that exact co-operation between the children and staff members. With such clarity it is possible to recognise and respond to individual differences between children. This separates the exceptional from the institutional – although the rules are for everyone, everyone is different. With recognition of individuals with their own particular talents, skills and needs, each child is expected to give to and can expect to receive from the group. The format is not pathology based but strength and performance based.

Our view is that no matter how damaging a child's experiences have been to their development, all children strive toward health. Power struggles between the child and the staff are not seen as productive. The programme format lays out the expectations and the staff assist the child through the programme. Although subtle, this idea of *assisting* children with their difficulties in the programme, rather than *requiring* compliance, is significant. As is the idea that the programme remains in the foreground of the interaction between worker and child, rather than the relationship between worker and child. This is not a discussion about 'feelings' for the staff in the traditional manner of 'I hear that you are angry at me now'. Rather, it is the question of 'How can I help you get to school now?' 'Would it be helpful to call your aunt? School is in 15 minutes. Probably you can be 30 minutes late today.' The emphasis rests with the child's competence and connections outside of the residence.

Much time and energy is spent in the planning, through weekly group meetings, shopping and preparation of food. In all programme activities, we find it essential to incorporate the child's family practices and preferences. Discussions with the child and group of children about their families brings out the uniqueness of each child.

The programme places the child's contact with their family as a right and not a privilege. If a child wants to call their family first thing in the morning, last thing at night, or anytime in between – they are encouraged to do so. The programme does not view children wanting to call their families as manipulative. Families and children must be free to call or visit at any time.

Dropping in is a good idea. Telephone times are built in at times convenient to the family, not to the programme. In fact there is nothing more important in the programme than the family.

Programme activities include the family. For example:

(a) Sibling nights and sibling groups which give room for the identified patient of the family to rejoin their own generation, away from the scrutiny and concern of the parental generation. By the time there is an admission, the siblings are usually as 'fed-up' as the parents with the behaviour of their brother or sister. Work with the sibling group of the family is very important for the future of the family as this generation outlives the parental generation and will either continue in an integrated fashion or will prematurely develop the beginnings of cut-offs.

(b) Parent groups for feedback about the programme and coffee for fellowship with each other and with the staff.

(c) Supper invitations for the family.

(d) Activity invitations. What would you like to invite your family to this week, discussed at the weekly activity planning meeting.

(e) Father/son events; mother/daughter events.

The main programming job is to make the residence accessible, welcoming and supportive to families for their full participation. The more isolated the programme becomes from the family, the more 'incident' reports are filed as the staff attempt to take over from the family during a period of increased isolation for the child.

The family

3. Families ask for residential services when all other resources have been exhausted or depleted. They feel helpless, furious, embarrassed at not being able to manage their child. Anger coupled with concern leads to a state of high anxiety, projections of blame and little hope for change. At the time of admission, the family has been like this for a long time – since the birth of the child for some. Most of the family interactions and thinking have been around the 'identified patient', their child. The family becomes totally organised around every move of the child – sleeping, eating, schooling and social life. All other family issues recede and are postponed.

4. The task of the therapy is to hear the story, find the strengths and the other 'set aside' issues. The child has become the 'field of packaging' for all other issues. These issues are complicated and have to do with loss, cut-off relationships, immigration, unemployment, divorce, dysfunctional marriages, violence, alcoholism. For whatever reason, the nuclear family has become the only family and is isolated with few resources.

The importance of the family story leads to the discovery of lost resources. The child is the foremost narrator of the story as they have been trying to help out the family by being the lightning rod. They will lead the therapist to the difficult areas:

> As the therapist asks about her grandmother and discovers that she lives in Scotland, she continues to follow the child's view of how her mother is doing so far away in Canada. Does she write or talk to her mother? When did she see her last? Will she see her again? How can she tell when her mother is sad? For how many years has she been sad?

> Your grandfather died? How difficult was that for your father? What do you think that he misses the most? How was that relationship with his father? Does he ever talk about this? Who is sadder? Your mother or your father? What is the marriage here? Whose side are you on? Whose side is your sister on? Do you ever trade sides?

Whatever the story: grandparents in Ghana, dead siblings of the parents, miscarriages, there is a bigger story than the child. The work begins with the alternate story – family of origin, loss, gendered power, economics. More people can be added to the sessions as consultants: friends and family creating an enlarged fabric with more flexibility and more possibilities for change. Family members become individuated and not the united mass they presented at admission. The therapy individuates them, divides them, subgroups them, genders them and makes crevices where they were all filled in.

The therapy should not be predictable or it will match the family. It needs to be surprising, confusing and constantly shifting. The programme needs to match this with a strong core of programming which can then be as flexible as the child needs to find a new place for themselves in their family.

The culture of the George Hull Centre has developed to include an expanded view of what is normal. Children and adolescents come to the Centre having experienced horrendous abuse, neglect and inconsistency in their care. Their attachments, behaviours and view of the world can be seen as quite disturbed. We prefer to view this as normal, given their experiences.

This opens up many more possibilities to intervene and provide new experiences from which children will grow.

For most children who have to leave their family for a period of time, there is the opportunity to return to a family which has reorganised to complete the child-rearing function. To capture this opportunity, there must be a strong ideology, from all levels and disciplines, that the family is the best place for the child with adequate support from the outside and work from the inside. Staff must embrace the disturbances of both the child and the family, knowing that these disturbances can be altered. Life need not be repetitive. The future can be different. This requires more than optimism – it requires well-trained staff. The Centre offers family therapy training to child and youth workers, as well as child and youth work training in residential work.

The uniqueness of treatment lies in the flexibility which comes from a strong programme. For example, with an eight-year-old girl who had been severely abused by the mother's partner and presented as a chronic runner, in mid-winter of a large metropolitan city, safety was a major concern; as was her attachment to her mother and her ongoing request that the mother take care of her, in increasingly difficult situations. The programme asked the mother to stay and sleep with her daughter at the residence. The mother agreed and the child stopped running. Even though she was the exception who could not return home to her mother's permanent care, the connection to the mother was strengthened to the extent that she could move to a long-term placement, knowing that the mother would be available to her, in her fashion.

Other examples include finding the 'lost' families from child welfare cases, where the child may have been separated from the family for many years. The reconnections may not facilitate return, but do facilitate a new stability to the child who has a family to visit and a connection beyond professional staff, who leave for their own families and Christmas.

For families who admit their child from home, unlike child welfare, the return requires an expansion of the family network, which produces more caretakers and more involvement with a community of friends, neighbours and extended kin. Some of these people are easily accessible; and when asked by the mother to come to a session, willingly attend and contribute new ideas and care to their friends, who are struggling. Others may live out of town. The cost to the Centre of bus or train tickets to interrupt the distance and isolation is small compared with the cost of long-term care.

This work is not for the faint-hearted. It is not short-term. It stops and starts again for many years. It requires staff who welcome back families when they get stuck again, not as failed, but as meeting at another point of their journey.

References

Andolfi, M., Angela, C. and deNicholo, M. (1989) *The Myth of Atlas: Families and the Therapeutic Story.* New York: Brunner/Mazel.

Minuchin, S. (1974) *Families and Family Therapy.* Cambridge, Massachusetts: Havard University Press.

Minuchin, S. (1984) *Family Kaleidoscope.* Cambridge, Massachusetts: Harvard University Press.

Minuchin, S., Montalvo, B., Guerney Jr, B; Rosman, B. and Schumer, F. (1967) *Families of the Slums: An Exploration of Their Structure and Treatment.* New York: Basic Books.

Napier, A and Whitaker, C. (1978) *The Family Crucible.* New York: Harper & Row.

Ridgely, E. (1994) The self of the consultant: "in" or "out"? In M. Andolfi and R. Haber (eds) *Please Help Me With This Family: Using Consultants as Resources in Family Therapy.* New York: Brunner/Mazel.

Ridgely, E. (1999) 'Family treatment.' In F.J. Turner (ed) *Social Work Practice: A Canadian Perspective.* Scarborough, Ontario: Prentice Hall Allyn and Bacon.

CHAPTER 7

The Family Group Home in Israel

Nechama Gluck

The 'Mifal' Educational Children's Homes and their context

This chapter discusses the role of 'Mifal' homes in Israel. These provide residential care for some 700 children aged 5–18, in six family group homes.

About 50,000 Israeli children aged 0–18 are being raised outside their homes. This figure includes private and élite boarding schools, religious institutions, and agricultural and military boarding schools. All these are normal educational alternatives. The Ministry of Welfare reported 7759 placements in residential care in July 1996. Of these, about 750 are in family group settings. An additional 1550 children are in foster care. The Ministry of Welfare Report did not include Mifal placements, which are offered mainly to children with serious family difficulties.

Israeli social welfare policy is to try to assist and rehabilitate malfunctioning families in a variety of ways so as to avoid placement outside the home. Such placement for a child under the age of 14 requires the decision of a special committee, to which the parents are also invited. Referral of a case to this committee is an indication that interventions with the family have failed or that the child's problems are too severe for the family to handle. This means that by the time the child reaches a Mifal home they have experienced much distress, frustration and failure. A growing number of children are referred by court order.

Each Mifal home comprises 6 to 20 family units. Each unit of 10–11 Mifal children aged 5–15 is cared for by a married couple (houseparents) living with their own biological children together with the Mifal children. Siblings are normally placed in the same unit.

The housemother is employed full-time. The housefather's official work hours are 17.00–21.00. He is expected to hold another job outside the home, thus providing a model of a working father. The housemother does not do domestic work: the central kitchen provides a hot lunch, laundry is

109

done centrally and cleaning staff are also provided. The housemother is thus able to devote most of her time to direct care of the children. These gender roles are admittedly somewhat conservative; however, we felt that the high incidence of unemployed malfunctioning biological fathers justified modelling a conventional working father role. The children are aware that the home is a place of employment for the houseparents. Thus the housemother is in fact also a working role model.

In addition to the Home Director, supporting staff include a home mother, social workers, psychologists, art therapists, tutors, and kitchen, laundry and maintenance personnel. A managing directorate assists and is responsible for setting and implementing 'Hamifal' policy. This directorate comprises chairman, supervisors, personnel manager, treasurer, head psychologist and social worker.

All day-to-day activities – meals, homework, leisure, etc. – take place within the unit. Supper is prepared together with the children, providing an educational and therapeutic experience in itself.

Children attend schools in the local community and participate in extracurricular activities within the home and in the community. Unless contraindicated, children visit their biological families every third weekend and for vacations. Families are encouraged to visit their children in the home.

Houseparents are trained to foster cooperation with the parents from the start. They are asked about their child's preferences, habits, dislikes, etc. They are assured that their role will continue to be central and crucial to their child's adjustment to the home and future development. Parents are kept informed of their children's progress as well as problems. Their consent is required for any educational, medical or psychological intervention. They are requested to keep the houseparents informed of any events which might affect daily functioning. The home social worker will try to establish a working relationship with the family, including a home visit, and encourage parents to confide information they might not want to share with the houseparents but which could be important for proper care of the child. Decisions concerning reunification are considered to be the responsibility of the referring authority, but they will normally be made in full cooperation with Mifal staff.

The family model – basic assumptions

The Mifal family model is based upon two assumptions:

1. Young children need to experience living within an adequately functioning family in order to internalise father, mother and sibling figures as part of their developing personality.

2. A child whose biological family does not provide an adequate family experience can benefit from a corrective surrogate one. A family unit led by a caring couple can make up for the inadequacy and provide positive parent role models, which in time will enable the child to establish a normal family of their own.

These assumptions are based on attachment theory. Carson (1988) claims that it is possible to remediate a distorted attachment caused by inadequate biological parenting. When the child is provided with reliable parent figures as in the home, they re-enact familiar, usually negative, patterns of behaviour. These provide the opportunity for the 'surrogate' parents to fulfil the child's longing for a caring parent figure who provides external control in a reassuring, nurturing manner. Thus a secure basis for a positive, satisfactory attachment is gradually formed.

Maier (1981) enumerated eight components essential for residential care:

1. *Rhythmic activities.* Continuous repetition induces a sense of permanency and predictability.

2. *Rituals.* Initiated by the children and supported by staff, rituals provide a form of psychological rhythm.

3. *Dependency.* A child's ability to rely on the care giver to fulfil basic needs enables the child to risk proceeding on their own, thus gradually developing independence. Support is available wherever this is required.

4. *Attachment.* Experience of developing a relationship through caring responses leads to close, loving relationships.

5. *Human contact and attention.* Sensitive responses to the child's need for attention, even when expressed in problematic ways, help the child build trust.

6. *Bodily comfort.* Small tokens of caring make the child feel wanted and welcome. (Examples include straightening sheets, offering a hot drink when child comes in from the cold, respecting privacy.)

7. *Transitional objects.* The child gains comfort from retaining prized possessions brought from home.

8. *Educational-behavioural programme.* Children learn most from persons significant to them, the primary caring persons.

The family model is a particularly effective framework for implementing these components in the day-to-day living situation. There are no work shifts and houseparents are constant figures living with the children.

A key advantage of the Mifal family group home is that responsibility for the children does not rest with the houseparents alone but is shared with the Home Director. Houseparents can consult with the home social worker or psychologist, as well as with their peers. They are free of domestic chores.

In the rest of this chapter, I would like to address several dilemmas which we have encountered during our 23 years experience with family group homes.

Dilemmas inherent in the family model

Houseparents who function well as a married couple and as biological parents will exert a direct and positive influence as houseparents as well. Children will gradually develop trust and attachment. The norms and expectations of the couples are then internalised and the children's functioning will tend to normalise in all areas. However, successful house-parents can inadvertently create in the children a conflict of loyalties between their feelings for them and for their biological parents. In addition, couples are frequently prone to stresses generated by guilt feelings towards their biological children if these are thought to receive less attention because of 'Mifal' children's needs, or towards 'Mifal' children if they receive less attention because of their biological children.

There is a grey area between the private life of the couple and their work obligations. Suppose, for example, a 12-year-old 'Mifal' child is asked to take care of the houseparents' baby – is this a family experience or exploitation?

Houseparents' private attitudes to childrearing are sometimes in conflict with those required by the home. They must then act in ways which are not congruent with their private attitudes. I recall one couple whose educational philosophy was one of *laissez-faire.* This couple was unperturbed by com-plaints from schools that the children in their care were not doing their homework and were undisciplined. The House Director demanded that the houseparents supervise the children's homework and behaviour. The house-parents told the children that they would have to shape up to the home's rules even though they, the houseparents, thought these rules were superfluous. In this case incongruence was explicit and the houseparents were eventually asked to leave. In other cases, incongruence will be less explicit but not necessarily less problematic.

Everything is done in order to recruit suitable couples but in practice it is sometimes necessary to compromise. If the couple does not function well, children may relive the disturbed functioning of their family of origin. The effect can be destructive.

A couple's work is intensive and therefore burnout symptoms will begin to appear sooner or later. When is it time to leave? At what cost to the children? Will they relive past experiences of rejection?

Dilemmas arising from application of the family model to an institutional setting

There would seem to be an inherent contradiction between the institutional system and the family system. The home includes such 'institutional' elements as central kitchen and laundry, ceremonies, official visits, volunteers, remedial teaching, organised afternoon recreational activities, psychologists and social workers. The houseparents are not autonomous in child management or in house management but must abide by home rules, budget, menus, etc.

In a family, the child usually learns to relate to their problems and solve them within the family. In the children's home they can turn to the Home Director, the home mother or the social worker to complain about the houseparents. The houseparents can also readily request help from the Home Director in solving discipline or other problems.

The houseparents require some privacy. Unlike most families, part of the family unit will therefore often be out of bounds for the children. Some of the houseparents' norms might well be unfamiliar to some of the children, causing them to feel 'different'.

When the houseparents and children do not 'click' despite professional intervention, there is a possibility of transferring the child to another unit, clearly not the case in a normal family. All these issues illustrate tensions in applying a family model within an institutional setting.

How does the Mifal deal with these dilemmas?

Our view is that despite the dilemmas of living with a surrogate mother figure, father figure and 'siblings', experiencing and building relationships with them in a family atmosphere will significantly contribute to the young child's normal development. They will benefit from the family experience even if it is not a pure and ideal one. However, the dilemmas must be recognised and dealt with as well as possible.

Clearly the Mifal cannot aspire to provide the child with an ideal alternative family. Houseparents cannot replace biological parents, but must be helped to accept the biological parents and – unless contraindicated – involve them in the child's life in the home. Houseparents must be regarded as an extension of the biological family (Watson 1982), partners to the parents in fulfilling the child's needs. Working together towards common objectives will reduce feelings of competition.

The institutional setting can actually lessen the conflict of loyalties faced by the child. The child is one of a group of children in the same situation and personal involvement with houseparents is somewhat less intensive than in a foster home.

Great effort is invested in recruiting suitable couples and providing them with in-service training. The recruitment process includes several meetings, psychological individual and group testing relating to personality, inter-personal and spouse relationships and a formal interview. At least two recommendations are required.

The issues which arise about the treatment of houseparents of biological children and their relationship with Mifal children is dealt with by clear rules, supervisory sessions and group discussion. Individual and group supervision for houseparents is important for ventilation of feelings and attitudes as well as for working out limits between private and work areas, autonomy and house rules. The Home Director and therapeutic staff are constantly on the alert to address problematic issues.

The departure of houseparents or other significant staff members is painful but it can provide a corrective experience of positively and openly handled leavetaking, in contrast to the often traumatic experience of the child leaving their biological home. The child is suitably prepared to cope with the parting. They are encouraged to express their feelings and house-parents are trained to acknowledge these feelings. Some positive contact will typically be maintained between the children and the houseparents after they have left.

Is the family model still relevant to children's needs today?

Present-day society includes a variety of parenting patterns, including single parents, couples and communes. Are we right in maintaining the traditional family model?

Current social welfare policy is to leave the child at home as long as possible. By the time they reach us they have experienced much distress, frustration and failure. Children are therefore more difficult to deal with – they are more aggressive and acting out, have more learning problems. More of them are known to have been abused. Is the family model still the most suitable for these children, or are more specialised staff indicated?

The Mifal is at present conducting a follow-up study of 118 of its former graduates, today aged 14–30. Preliminary results show that most graduates experienced their Mifal placements as warm and caring, as well as helping them significantly in most areas of development: school, social skills, family, military service and employment. Ninety-one per cent of these graduates are currently at school, doing military service or employed.

We believe that children's basic needs have not changed. Although single-parent families are today considered quite normal, we believe that every child still needs to internalise positive figures of both sexes, and a long-term positive relationship between them. However, we do find that today this basis is no longer enough but must be quite heavily reinforced by professional care. Each child's individual needs are assessed and every effort is made to meet them and so to contribute to their development as a whole person. Among the major needs are the following:

1. *Educational needs.* Acquisition of learning habits, making up for lost ground, overcoming learning difficulties, attention and concentration problems. All these require specialised teachers trained in these areas.

2. *Developmental needs.* Some children will require specialist services such as speech therapy, occupational therapy, etc.

3. *Emotional needs.* Robinson (1987) describes removal of a child from their family as a process of mourning including stages of denial, fear of the new environment and sometimes physical and behavioural symptoms, complaints, clinging, temper tantrums and guilt feelings. Helping the child to work through the mourning process will enable them to cope with this experience more easily. New children are encouraged to express their feelings in small groups through a structured series of meetings. The local staff will subsequently decide which children need further professional intervention or treatment.

4. *Social needs.* The family group is a firm base from which the child
   can branch out to social ties with children in other groups and in
   the general community. The child is encouraged to integrate in the
   community, personally and through organised activities.

Social norms within the home are spelled out clearly. Children are
encouraged to develop responsibility for their actions. They learn through
group discussions that each child has rights and is entitled to respect and
protection. A clear social-educational model of behaviour can correct
negative or confused messages received within the child's family. A
structured programme provides the child with assertive ways of dealing with
threats of abuse both from children and from adults.

All these interventions require intensive training both for couples and for
professional staff. This is provided both within and outside the homes.

In summary, the family model, reinforced by specialist auxiliary services,
is our model of choice for providing optimal residential care for young
children.

References

Carson, M.L. (1988) 'The children's garden attachment model.' In R. Small (ed)
    Challenging the Limits of Care. Needham, MA: Trieschman Center.

Maier, H. (1981) ' Essential components in care and treatment environments for
    children.' In F. Ainsworth (ed) *Group Care For Children.* London: Tavistock.

Robinson, M.R. (1987) 'Reconstituted families.' In A. Bentovim and G. Barnes (eds)
    Family Therapy. London: Academic Press.

Watson, K.W. (1982) 'A bold new model for foster family care.' *Public Welfare 40,*
    14–21.

CHAPTER 8

Family Reconstitution and the Implications for Group Care Workers: An American Perspective

Irene Stevens

Introduction

This chapter will review the evidence about the significance of family reconstitution. It will go on to look at a specific programme developed in Boston that will enable residential workers to tackle some of these issues as they relate to the young people in their care.

During the 1970s there was a massive increase in the number of divorces in the UK. In 1978, 143,700 decrees were made absolute, as compared with 45, 800 in 1968 (Office of Population and Census Surveys 1979). This trend has continued, so that about one in three marriages is a remarriage for at least one parent. Additionally, there are many previously married people who come together in cohabitation relationships which do not appear in the official statistics. The picture painted for the success of a remarriage or second relationship remains poor, with Maddox (1980) indicating that a remarriage is twice as likely to break down as a first marriage. As a residential child care worker in Britain between 1984 and 1989, I was struck by the number of young people coming into my unit who were from a reconstituted family. Over 60 per cent of referrals to our unit were from young people in step-families. Yet often this fact was not deemed to be significant. John Cran, the manager of my unit, encouraged me to look into this in more detail. I followed up the interest by undertaking some research into the area as part of an MSc programme. Like many residential workers I did not realise how *different* the stepfamily experience was from that of the traditional nuclear family. Additionally I came to recognise that the reconstituted family labours under the ideology of the 'normal' family to which it always tries to aspire. I continued this interest and, in early 1995, I travelled to America on a Churchill Fellowship to look at work with stepfamilies in the USA and Canada.

The North American context

Before looking at some of the work with stepfamilies in North America, it is important to understand two major contextual factors. These factors help us to see why particular advances have been made in the USA and Canada. Some of these advances have application for residential workers in Britain and elsewhere.

Public provision in North America, especially the USA, differs considerably from that in Western European welfare states:

1. Hence the funding of help for stepfamilies was different from Britain. There was a flourishing private practice in the provision of help for families. The families either paid for this themselves or it was funded through insurance schemes. This means that specialist services have grown and developed spurred on by commercialism and competition.

2. In the field of stepfamily work, I could identify no services provided by professional voluntary organisations, which provide a major part of family support services in the UK. This in turn has led to the development of a flourishing culture of self-help groups which run along 'non-profit-making' lines.

Stepfamily structure: Some points for consideration

Osborne (1983) identified a very helpful way of visualising the restructuring process of the reconstituted family in terms of six stages. The important point for residential child care workers to understand is that a young person may be caught in the dynamics of one or more of these stages. Also the residential worker may have to help the child to resolve not only the issues arising from reception into care but also the issues left over from the life stage of their family. Osborne's stages are:

1. *Fantasy.* The adults and the young people in the new family have fantasies about how things are going to be. The adult fantasies are almost always positive. The young people's fantasies are generally more mixed. Those with positive fantasies will feel like insiders. Those with negative fantasies will feel like outsiders.

2. *Pretending.* This is where participants pretend to be a normal family and work hard at trying to appear normal to the outside world. However, 'normal' is just whatever the prevailing ideology of the family is at that time.

3. *Panic.* This is where one or more people in the family recognise and own their view of the family and of other family members as different. The mask of the family is blown away. There is a sense of lack of control and helplessness as the family reinvents itself as closer to reality.

4. *Conflict.* The family, or individuals within it, confront differences in values and approaches. The needs of each person must be clarified and limits set around the issues causing conflict.

5. *Reworking.* Conflict begins to be resolved in new and different ways. New and more workable relationships between adults, and between parents and children, need to be evolved.

6. *Moving on.* There is a clear awareness that the step relationships are different from the original child–parent relationships. These relationships, based on a true affinity, now have a chance to grow and develop or to lead to a realisation that the relationship is untenable and should end.

When you view the stepfamily structure in this way, then as a residential worker you have a better chance to understand the dynamics of some receptions into care. Engaging with step-relationships may occur at three levels (Papernow 1993):

1. *The personal.* Either with the individual adults or the individual children involved.

2. *The couple.* With the biological parent and the step-parent together.

3. *The stepfamily.* With the family group as a whole.

Issues facing young people from stepfamilies

Visher and Visher (1979) indicated that the pressures on the newly reconstituted family can be enormous. These can include:

- The child or young person has a biological parent who lives elsewhere. Although statistics indicate that this is becoming a more common occurrence, the child in that situation can feel isolated, frightened and guilty about this.

- The parent–child relationship predates the new adult partnership between parent and step-parent. This means that the child or young person is unaware of the expectations of the new adult, which may be very different from those of the natural parent. Similarly, the new adult 'intrudes' on a history that exists between the child and their biological parent. This may lead to the new adult feeling left out. This, in turn, can lead to them blaming the child for the problems.

- Virtually all members of the new family have sustained a primary loss. The children have suffered the loss of a parent. The biological parent will, in all likelihood, have lost a previous relationship. Loss is accompanied by stages of grieving. The children in these relationships may be trying to resolve grief. Ironically, the people they depend on to help the most (i.e. their parents) may not be emotionally or physically able to give their children the support they require.

All of these issues have implications for practice in residential care. The residential worker can sometimes be at a loss to understand the rage and frustration of the child in care. The child him- or herself comes to be seen as the problem. However, if there are unresolved grief issues as well as stepfamily issues to be worked on, it can help the residential worker to understand the child in a deeper way. Clearly, the importance of detailed case history is important, to enable the worker to see some of the issues which may not even be apparent to the child or their family. I believe that an understanding of the structure and the issues facing stepfamilies in general can help the residential worker to provide a better service to the young people in their care. The points outlined by Visher and Visher provide an invaluable context in which the residential workers can frame their interventions with the child and their family.

The New Families Programme

The New Families Programme is run by Alexandra Erikson in Boston, Massachusetts. She ran a series of groups with children and young people of different ages, to help them come to terms with family reconstitution. I believe that the programme has great relevance for residential workers as it embraces a range of techniques that may be used in group situations.

The groups are clearly structured, using age-appropriate methods based on Piaget's stages of intellectual development (Roth 1991). The groups run for 10 weeks and the young people within the group are encouraged to share thoughts and feelings about divorce and remarriage-related topics. Goals of the programme focus on giving children and young people information, normalising their experiences, developing appropriate coping skills and enhancing their self-esteem.

Younger children are encouraged to use drawings and games to express their feelings. Older children are encouraged to write, discuss and enter into role plays. The use of these techniques has developed from using child-centred understanding of the issues. Kalter (1990), on whose work the New Families Programme is based, points out stressors in the lives of children in a reconstituted family. These include:

- competitive feelings towards the step-parent for the time and affection of the parent

- complicated loyalties between their positive feelings about the step-parent and the absent parent

- anger toward the parent and step-parent for interfering in the wish for reconciliation between the child's biological parents

- resentment over the step-parent exercising authority over which he or she is seen to have no legitimate claim, for example, assigning chores or handing down discipline

- difficulties in relationships with step-siblings.

Kalter points out that the prevailing model of intervention for children of divorce and remarriage is based on a 'crisis intervention' view where damage is limited if the intervention is immediate or as soon as possible after the event. However, as he also states, there are long-term psychological tasks which have to be addressed by children and young people as well. Some of the issues dealt with by residential workers may have their roots in the past through unresolved issues around a marital breakdown.

Some of the techniques used by Erikson in the New Families Programme include encouraging young people to jointly write a newsletter about the processes of divorce and remarriage. They role play issues like pre-divorce fights, or arguments with a step-parent. This is helpful in allowing the young people to express and analyse their feelings. Drawing life line peaks and troughs to represent the good and bad times is helpful in focusing on the positive as well as on the negative aspects of their lives. Setting up a panel of 'divorce experts' like a game show is also a useful technique to get young people talking.

The success rate of the programme was measured by follow-up interviews with the children and parents. It was generally found that attendance at the group had been helpful and children felt much better about themselves and more in control than before.

A model of work for group care workers

Look at your own unit and the young people in your care. Are there any young people from a reconstituted family background? A reconstituted family can be loosely defined as one where the child lives with two adults, one of whom is not their biological parent. Having looked at the particular issues that are around for these young people, you may want to build in some work around the issue of family reconstitution. This model reflects a groupwork approach but you can also adopt parts of it for one-to-one keyworker sessions with individual young people in your care. As always, with any discrete groupwork within a group care environment, you should prepare the workplace for the running of the group and ensure that the same facilitators are on shift each time. These facilitators should be familiar with some of the issues likely to be raised as outlined in this chapter. The group should run for six weeks with a session lasting one hour. A good ratio in the group is 6–8 young people and two adults. There should be equal gender representation if possible and age difference should be no more than a year.

The six sessions should be organised as follows:

Week one

Exploration of the aims and objectives of the group. Rule setting. Each young person charts up their family tree or life line on a large sheet of paper. This is compared to others and discussed. Workers should start off the exercise by sharing their own family tree.

Week two

The idea of a group story is introduced. The young people are asked to make up and write a story together. Everyone has a part in writing or drawing the story. It will be the story of a divorce and a new relationship. It will be written and illustrated by the young people for other young people in a similar situation. This will involve discussion of who does what and negotiation about process as well as content.

Week three

Dealing with arguments is looked at here. The two group leaders role play an argument between two parents which leads to one of them leaving. This is then used to help the young people in the group express their feelings about arguments and fighting. Then the two group leaders role play two children who have heard their parents fighting. They talk about their feelings (anger, guilt, fear, helplessness, sadness). Then the group is encouraged to share any feelings they had and how they coped with them. The feelings are then charted on large sheets of paper and worked on to produce a set of helpful tips for young people to deal with their feelings.

Week four

The concept of a step-parent is introduced. The two group leaders role play a parent telling their child that there may be a new man or woman in their lives, and that he or she is coming to stay. The group then discuss any feelings they had about this situation or how it happened for them. They are asked to draw a picture of their feelings about this. The pictures are pinned up and used for discussion.

Week five

A game called 'Divorce and Stepfamily Experts' is set up. Here the group leaders play the 'experts'. The group gets together to decide the type of questions they want to put to the panel.

Week six

The group compiles the 'Divorce and New Family' newspaper. It should help to summarise and integrate the issues which have emerged in the course of the group meetings. The group may interview each other around the topic of family breakdown and reconstitution from short articles. They may take pictures to illustrate feelings, or a group picture to indicate the 'editorial' group. They may incorporate a problem page, helpful hints on how to deal with feelings and answers from the 'divorce experts'. They should be encouraged to design a format for the newspaper. Tasks should be evenly divided up. The production of the newspaper is a good way to end the group as it gives everyone something to go away with.

These group sessions should be carried out by experienced group care workers and should follow basic groupwork rules. Individual debriefing is needed. If any young person wants to work on a particular issue with their keyworker, they should be encouraged to do this. The topics and issues discussed above have clear implications for family work and family contact issues. If the family is maintaining contact with the young person, and there is a chance that the young person may return home, then the family should be involved in discussing any particular issues for the young person. This may involve the family examining themselves in a way that has never happened before. In particular, it means having to accept some very uncomfortable feelings and acknowledging that the young person has a right to their feelings. Also the young person has a right to express these feelings appropriately to the family. Any keyworker involved in these activities should keep this in mind and prepare both the family and the young person for the discussion of these feelings.

Conclusion

Residential child care workers should have an overall picture of the effects of family reconstitution when working with the young people in their care. The responsibility is on the workers to update their knowledge and to be ready to implement ways of working which may be new to them. By having a clear picture of the young person and of reconstitution issues, the worker is empowered to work proactively.

All too often, residential workers feel that they are reacting to issues which seem to be largely outwith their control. However, by opening up the issues, and understanding about the profound ongoing effects of family breakdown and reconstitution, the worker can actively help the young people in their care to come to terms with painful aspects of their lives and move on. This chapter has outlined a few of the issues and gives some ideas about how to work with them. However, I would encourage workers to look to their own skills and their own ideas and develop other imaginative ways of working. The benefits for the young people in our care will be worth it.

References

Kalter, N. (1990) *Growing Up with Divorce.* New York: Ballantine Books.

Maddox, B. (1980) *Step-parenting.* London: Unwin.

Office of Population and Census Surveys (1979) Marriage and Divorce Statistics. London: HMSO.

Osborne, J. (1983) *Stepfamilies: The Restructuring Process.* Boston: Stepfamily Associates.

Papernow, P. (1993) *Becoming a Stepfamily.* San Francisco: Jossey Bass.

Roth, I. (1991) *Introduction to Psychology.* Buckingham: Open University Press.

Visher, E.B. and Visher, J.S. (1979) *Stepfamilies: Myths and Realities.* New York: Citadel Press.

CHAPTER 9

Role of Siblings in Relation to Children in Residential Care

Marjut Kosonen

Children's relationships with their sisters and brothers have received little attention compared with their relationships to parents. It could be argued that this is because the focus of residential care continues to centre on children's relationships with adults. The significance of children's relationships with other children including siblings, friends and peers is little understood by practitioners, carers and policy-makers.

One of the primary concerns for residential care practice has been the maintenance of children's relationships with their parents, most commonly their mothers. Yet over 80 per cent of children in out-of-home placements in the United Kingdom have siblings (Kosonen 1996a). Little research evidence exists regarding how children define their families, who they regard as their siblings and how they perceive their relationships with their sisters and brothers. Research studies focusing on children's care experiences suggest that siblings continue to hold an importance in the children's lives.

This chapter discusses sibling relationships for children in residential care in the context of research relating to children's relationships with their sisters and brothers in general. Some of the findings of a study of the perceptions of 64 9–12-year-old children on their siblings are presented, followed by a discussion on the implications of the study for residential care policy and practice. The chapter argues that more attention should be paid by residential care workers to the children's sibling relationships in the here and now, as well as for the sake of the children's long-term welfare.

Why are sibling relationships unique?

Sibling relationships are different from the child's other relationships in a number of ways. There is no choice in the relationship, unlike in relationships with friends and peers. It has been imposed on the child by his or her circumstance of being born or living in a particular family. Sibling relationships are also characterised by a diversity of siblingship form or type. Children may be full or half-siblings, sharing one or both of their biological parents; or step-siblings where they are united by their parents' marital status or cohabitation and often common living arrangements. Children may also acquire siblings by social and legal arrangements through adoption and fostering, where the relationship with a sibling has psychological and social meaning rather than a biological one. Additionally, children may live with their siblings, or live apart from one or more of them, creating a variety of patterns of relationships, depending on the residence status, amount of contact and other factors. Treffers *et al.* (1990) identified no less than 26 different patterns of siblingship in their study of children attending child and adolescent psychiatry clinics.

What sense do children make of such complex siblingship arrangements? There is dearth of information available about children's views on their siblings and less so of whom they regard as their sisters and brothers. Morgan (1980) in his discussion on the social definition of family suggests that '...some considerable account must be taken of the actor's own definitions of the boundaries of his family and the way in which these boundaries might vary according to context or situation. The actor's definition of the family is not a once and for all accomplishment but a continuous process of creation and redefinition' (p.345).

The process of change which individual families undergo, as members of the family leave or new members join, leads to restructuring of family relationships. A child may belong to and live in more than one family during childhood. Simpson (1994) draws attention to the complex restructuring of kinship arrangements which can occur following divorce and remarriage; he refers to such restructured families as 'unclear families'.

Sibling relationships are also unique in being diverse in nature and quality, compared with friendships which are often characterised by mutual trust, affection and support (Dunn and McGuire 1992). Some sibling relationships may manifest mutual liking, sharing, support and co-operation, whereas others may be marked by antagonism, hostility, dislike and a high degree of conflict. Many sibling relationships are characterised by ambivalence, including both positive and negative features.

Children also develop qualitatively different relationships with different siblings, depending on their position in the family, their own and a sibling's gender, proximity in age to a sibling, temperament, experiences in their family and other factors. Consequently the meaning of sibling experience is likely to be unique for each child in the family.

Sibling relationships for children in out-of-home care

Children in out-of home placements face a number of difficulties in developing and maintaining relationships with their sisters and brothers. They may have experienced a number of changes of family composition and living situation prior to entering care. The findings of research in the UK into children's care experiences suggest that changes in family composition and living situation continue to take place following a child's entry into care. Such changes in the children's own and their families' lives can lead to separation from, reduced contact with or total loss of contact with sisters and brothers (Millham et al. 1986; Farmer and Parker 1991; Bullock, Little and Millham 1993). Children are particularly vulnerable to separation from their siblings at the point of entering or leaving residential or foster care. Where children are separated at the point of entry into care, there are rarely plans for reuniting them following separation (Kosonen 1996a). The changes which affect children in residential care impact on the children's relationships with siblings and other members of their families. Morgan's (1980) paradigm of family suggests that particular attention should be paid to the children's own views on the boundaries of their families in the context of changes taking place in the child's situation.

There is also growing evidence from research into children's sibling relationships which suggests that children in out-of-home placements have potential for developing problematic relationships with their sisters and brothers. Kosonen (1994) in a literature review identified certain family background features shared by many children in out-of-home placements, which also characterise problematic sibling relationships. Such background features include: insecure attachments; poor parental relationship; family conflict, stress and hostility; neglect and abuse; and physical and/or emotional parental unavailability.

In contrast, studies into sibling relationships for children in the general population suggest that sibling relationships, although marked by ambivalence and conflict, are experienced by children during middle childhood and adolescence as primarily positive (Boer 1990; Buhrmester and Furman 1990).

What do children in out-of-home care say about their siblings?

Sibling relationships for children in residential and foster care have rarely been the focus of study in their own right. Where primary research interest has been on siblings, this has focused on placement or contact with siblings rather than the nature and quality of sibling relationships (MacLean 1991; Wedge and Mantle 1991; Bilson and Barker 1992/93). There is little empirical evidence regarding how children in residential care define their families, who they regard as their siblings and how they perceive their relationships with their sisters and brothers.

A number of qualitative studies into children's placement experiences using interviews with children (Weinstein 1960; Thorpe 1980; Rowe *et al.* 1984; Whitaker *et al.* 1984; McAuley 1996) have found that the continuity of sibling relationships is of great benefit to children's well-being and adjustment and that children themselves valued being placed with or maintaining contact with their sisters and brothers. A study by Whitaker *et al.* (1984) of children in residential care found that children who were placed with their siblings 'acknowledged quarrelling and other difficulties, but at the same time saw their siblings as a source of support and protection, ' and that a significant number of children who were separated from their siblings 'struggled with feelings of loss, frustration and bewilderment, sometimes years after the separation took place' (p.14).

McAuley (1996) in her recent study of children in long-term foster care found that children continued to be preoccupied with their separated birth siblings, by frequently thinking or dreaming about them. She suggests that '... contact was very important to these children and seemed to compensate for lack of contact with parents at times by maintaining a sense of family identity. The sense from the children was that they had travelled through troubled times together' (p.158).

A study by Buchanan *et al.* (1993) of the views of young people on their care experiences found that 'when in care they wanted the option to be with their brothers and sisters' and that 'most young people knew whether they wanted contact with their family and wanted their views respected ...' (p.51). The findings of another survey by the Who Cares? Trust and the National Consumer Council suggest that contact with siblings living at home or in foster care was difficult to maintain for young people in residential care (Fletcher 1993).

Stein and Carey's (1986) study of the views of care leavers found that where there were difficulties in maintaining closeness with parents, siblings became more important to young people and that contact with separated siblings was re-established after leaving care where siblings could be found.

Young people who had lost contact with their families expressed 'varying degrees of ignorance, sadness, resentment and bitterness about lost or hardly known parents and siblings' (p.118).

The research that has explored the views of children living in residential or foster care supports the notion that siblings continue to retain a long-term importance for children living away from their families. Little research evidence exists regarding the views of children in the general population in the UK on their sisters and brothers. The study described in this chapter was undertaken to explore the views of children in the general population on their relationships with their siblings.

A Scottish study

A questionnaire survey of children's views on their siblings was undertaken in a Scottish city. The sample was drawn by including all children in three primary school classes in three different schools. Two of the schools served socio-economically disadvantaged urban housing schemes.

The sample consisted of 69 children, of whom 64 had one or more siblings. Five children defined themselves as only children. Some of the findings relating to the children with siblings are presented here.

The sample of children who had siblings comprised 38 (59.4%) girls and 26 (40.6%) boys. Children were aged 9 (33%), 10 (34%), 11 (30%) and 12 (3%). Thirty-six per cent of the children who had siblings had one sibling, 28 per cent had two, 19 per cent had three and 17 per cent had four or more siblings. The children reported a total of 152 siblings, averaging 2.4 siblings per child. The study population contained larger than average families.

A questionnaire was developed with a help of a group of local children, to take account of the particular context of a Scottish city. The first part of the questionnaire had mainly open-ended questions relating to siblings in general; the second part that was based on a questionnaire by Furman (1990) sought out the children's views about their individual siblings. Only some of the findings relating to the first part of the questionnaire are presented here. Readers may refer to an article by the author (Kosonen 1996b) for a discussion on some of the other findings.

Children and their families

The study used as a starting point children's own definitions of their family composition, including their definition of a 'sibling'. Subsequently, some children omitted their biological siblings living away from the family home, while others included foster siblings living temporarily with the family.

The children came from diverse types of families, ranging from one parent and one child, to two-parent families with up to seven children, all living in the family home. Some children came from complex family backgrounds, having different types of siblings living in a number of family situations.

Separation from family members was relatively common. The children lived permanently separated not only from one of their parents, but also from their siblings. Nearly one-third of the children mentioned one or more family members who lived away from home; this included 27 per cent of the children's siblings. The majority of children said that they missed their siblings 'a lot' or 'quite a lot' when separated even for short periods of time; only eight children said they did not miss their siblings at all.

Children, siblings and friends

By middle childhood children's social worlds encompass relationships with adults and other children outside their immediate family. In order to place children's views about their siblings in the context of a wider network of relationships within the family, school, neighbourhood and the community, information was sought about the children's friendship networks and to what extent these were shared with sisters and brothers. Older siblings in particular serve a useful function in introducing younger siblings to other children outside the family home.

The study children were asked about friends and whether these were shared by their siblings. When the number of joint friends were considered it was found that nearly two-thirds of the children shared some joint friends with their siblings. Almost a third (30%) shared 1–2 friends with their siblings, 22 per cent mentioned 3–5 joint friends, and eight children had at least 6 joint friends. The joint friendships were only maintained between siblings who were living together. Separation of siblings potentially reduces the child's friendship network, making it difficult for a child to maintain joint friendships with their siblings.

Comparing siblings and friends

During middle childhood friends become increasingly important to children. Children spend more time with other children at school than with their siblings, who were often their main companions during pre-school years. Are there any differences in the way children perceive their siblings and friends? Children were asked to describe how they perceived these differences.

One-third of the children had a clear concept of siblings as being part of their family, whom they love and care about. Children described these differences as: 'They are family and I love them'; 'They care about you because they are family.' The difference in closeness to siblings was explained by greater affectionate ties, such as: 'They love me and my friends like me' and 'You can tell them things you cannot tell your friends' and in terms of kinds of resources exchanged: 'Your family gives you money and sweets and your friends only give sweets.'

Over a quarter of the children attributed differences between siblings and friends to getting on better with their friends, with whom they had less conflict. They found their friends more cooperative, helpful and supportive. This group of children also preferred to play with their friends. Children described this by saying: 'My friends are much nicer than my brother and sister'; 'My friends help me when I am hurt and my brothers and sisters don't'; and 'Usually my friends don't shout at me.'

The third group of children described the differences between siblings and friends in terms of having greater familiarity with their siblings as a result of living with them and growing up together. One of the study children described the difference by saying: 'I love my sister and see her every day and I like my friends and see them five days'; another by saying: 'You see more of your brothers and sisters' and 'I have known my brothers and sisters longest.'

A few children found little in common with their siblings, who were disparate in age or had different interests and tastes. They had more in common with their friends.

Siblings were perceived by the study children to provide a sense of family identity, closeness and warmth. This was balanced by conflict between the child and siblings. Friends were perceived as their greatest source of companionship.

The findings accord with a study of children's social networks by Furman and Buhrmester (1985), who found sibling relationships, in contrast to children's relationships with their parents, grandparents, friends and teachers, to be most commonly characterised by conflict.

What are sisters and brothers really like?

By middle childhood children require less direct supervision by their parents. As children become more independent, their relationships with their sisters and brothers can be less effectively monitored by parents, and they may take a different direction when parental management is not present (Bank and Kahn 1975). Little is known in research terms about what goes on between sisters and brothers outside parental view. The private world of siblings often remains out of reach to parents and other adults. How do we know what sisters and brothers are really like? A questionnaire was developed to explore children's views on a range of issues including their position in the family, sibling care taking and parental favouritism.

In the study children were asked to describe what they liked most and least about their sisters and brothers, and what their ideal, perfect sister and brother would be like. Despite a general nature of the questions many children responded by stating what they liked most and least about their individual siblings. Their responses revealed that the children had an ability to recognise the unique characteristics of each sibling and the different roles siblings play in their lives.

Children had more positive than negative things to say about their siblings. A total of 105 statements were made about the most liked characteristics compared with 70 statements about the least liked features. Children's statements generally contained more than one characteristic. These were attributed to different siblings as siblings were liked and disliked for different reasons.

What do children like most about their siblings?

The following themes emerged as the most positive aspects of sibling experiences:

- Siblings provide fun and company
- They are kind
- They offer help and support
- They provide services and resources
- They love you.

A small minority (15%) could not think of anything positive to say about their siblings or framed the response in terms of a lack of negative interactions, for example, 'when they don't hit me.' The children's perceptions are explored in more detail below.

SIBLINGS ARE FUN AND PLAY WITH YOU

Sisters and brothers were seen as an easily available source of fun and play for 41 per cent of the children. Playing with siblings and having fun with them was mentioned most often by the children. Children were also aware of a sibling meeting a need in them, as a response by a middle child illustrates: 'She plays with me if I need fun.' Playing with siblings was seen as a fun thing to do: 'They like the same things I do, they are fun to play with' and 'They're funny, they're thick, they're mental, they're dumb,' said a youngest brother of his older siblings.

SIBLINGS ARE KIND

Sisters and brothers who were kind to the children were valued by the study children. Thirty-nine per cent of the children mentioned kindness as the characteristic they valued most about their siblings. Some of the children did not elaborate on what they meant by kindness beyond stating: 'When he is kind to me'; 'They are kind and like me'; 'They are kind – all right sometimes'.

Most of the children perceived kindness in terms of their siblings giving them things, such as money and sweets. The siblings' generosity was appreciated by the children, who said: 'Kind – give me loads of stuff'; 'Laura she gives me things, Tom he is cute'; 'Gives me money and spoils me'. One of the children made a distinction between sibling kindness and parental love by stating the following about his younger sister: 'She gives me money all the time and she is kind and my cat gives me scratches and my mum gives me food and love'.

SIBLINGS HELP AND SUPPORT YOU

Sisters' and brothers' role as 'helpers' to the children was recognised by over a quarter of the study children (28%). Helping was described as taking a number of forms: helping with school work, advice on relationships and emotional support. What these children liked most about their siblings was that: 'She always helps me on my maths if I have to take it home'; 'If I am upset she always comes to my aid'; 'They help me about my boyfriend'; and 'They sometimes help me when I am sad or hurt'; 'They help me when I am getting bullied'. Some children valued being able to share their thoughts with and being listened to by their siblings, as described by a girl about her much older sister: 'I like Shelly because I could talk to her unlike my mum'. Older siblings in particular were perceived as a significant source of support and help.

SIBLINGS PROVIDE SERVICES AND RESOURCES

Siblings were valued as providers of a range of services and resources by a quarter of the study children. These included being allowed to borrow siblings' belongings, play with their toys, gain access to a computer and being taken by siblings to places the children could not go by themselves.

Borrowing and sharing the belongings of older siblings was most common, although some of the oldest children also valued the exchange of resources with their younger siblings. The following responses describe the pleasure children get from such exchange of resources among the siblings: 'He lets me go on his computer'; 'He lets me hold his hamster'; 'My sister lets me have her earrings'; 'I get to play with their toys'; and 'She gives me a shot of her CDs and cassettes'.

SIBLINGS LOVE YOU

Being loved by your sisters and brothers was mentioned by 19 per cent of the children. Sibling love was described simply as: 'They love me, care for me'; 'They are very loving and play with me every day'; 'They help me and love me'.

What do children like least about their siblings?

When asked to describe what the children liked least about their siblings, 10 children (16%) responded by saying there was nothing they disliked about their sisters and brothers or used a positive statement such as: 'My sister is nice to me' and 'My brother is good'. Seven of the children with the most positive view of their siblings were middle or oldest children in their family.

The following themes reveal children's perceptions of the most negative aspects of the sibling experience:

- Siblings are annoying
- They abuse you
- They fight
- They misuse their power
- Lack of privacy.

SIBLINGS ARE ANNOYING

One-third of the children described their sisters and brothers as 'annoying'. Most children, however, did not define what constituted annoying behaviour. The term 'annoying' simply described the most commonly negatively perceived sibling characteristics.

The children described their siblings in the following terms: 'They annoy me;' 'They always annoy you;' 'When they annoy me'. Some children were more specific about what they found annoying about their siblings: 'My sister is so stubborn;' 'Sometimes they are a pain'. Moaning and shouting by siblings was found be annoying, as illustrated by the following responses: 'Sometimes she is a moaner;' 'Jemma moans all the time;' 'Sometimes moans for nothing at me'.

SIBLINGS ABUSE YOU

Some children were subject to a range of abusive behaviour from their sisters and brothers. Fourteen children (22%) found sibling abuse the most disliked aspect of the sibling experience. The abuse described by the study children took a variety of forms ranging from verbal abuse such as calling names, to physical abuse by hitting, scratching, kicking, punching, etc. The children most commonly reporting abuse were the youngest and middle children in the family.

Children's responses describe their experiences of abuse: 'She hits, punches and kicks me and it is sore;' 'They call me names and hit me;' Jack screams, Kelly scratches me with her knuckles. He always hits me;' 'He always pushes me;' 'One of my sisters can batter me;' and 'She always scratches and nips me'.

SIBLINGS FIGHT

Sibling fighting with the study children was disliked by 9 (14%) of the 64 children. The children described their feelings by saying: 'When we fight I hate it'; 'They argue with me and sometimes fight with me;' 'Well I always have fights with them.' It was not the fighting on its own which the children disliked most, but not winning or being left out, as one of the youngest children described of her brother: 'When we fight he always wins,' and another child: 'They fight and leave me out.' A surprisingly small proportion of children disliked their siblings *because* they fight. The children indicated that it is the outcome of the fight, when the child gets hurt or upset or does not win, which is more disliked than the fighting itself.

SIBLINGS MISUSE THEIR POWER

Domination and power exercised by the siblings over the study children in terms of being able to get them in trouble, tell on them, preventing them from doing things or not letting them borrow things was mentioned by a minority of children (12.5%). Children complained of such misuse of power regardless of their own position in the family. Both older and younger siblings were disliked for this reason: 'She takes the computer off me and does not let me hold her hamster;' 'Never giving me a shot of new games;' 'They always tell on me when I did not do a thing;' 'She always takes my TV and gets me in trouble ...' describe the children's feelings of their siblings.

LACK OF PRIVACY

Some children found having sisters and brothers around intrusive and distracting. Although only a small proportion of children described lack of privacy as the most disliked feature of their sibling experiences, their responses are powerful and give an insight into the complexity of children's relationships with their siblings. Children said about their siblings: 'I hate my sister when she distracts me from what I want to do;' 'I least like my brother, when he comes into my room, when I do not want him in it;' 'They wake me up when I am sleeping;' 'They wake me up early on Saturday and Sunday.' Children's views on the most and least liked sibling characteristics demonstrate a spectrum of positive and negative features prevalent in sibling relationships.

Although primarily positive, sibling relationships are also characterised by a high degree of conflict and ambivalence, confirming previous research in North America (Furman and Buhrmester 1985; Buhrmester and Furman 1990) and in Holland (Boer 1990). Sibling relationships are clearly paradoxical in nature and not always easy to untangle.

How did the children view their relationships with their siblings in the long term?

Siblings inevitably become part of the life experiences of those who have them. Research into sibling relationships in adulthood suggests that most people retain some links with their siblings throughout their lifetime and that it is rare for siblings to lose contact with each other (Cicirelli 1982).

How do children view their sibling relationships in the long term; and what expectations do they hold of the future?

The findings indicate that the children hold clear expectations of the role their siblings will play in their lives in the future. The majority of children said they expect to live close to their siblings; to maintain frequent contact with them; to have a number of joint activities' and have fun together in the future. Children wished to live near to their siblings and see them frequently, regardless of their current living situation. Even the separated siblings were perceived to retain an importance in the children's lives in the future. By far the majority of children (77%) said they wanted to see their siblings 'often', 17 per cent 'not often' and only 4 per cent would 'never' like to see their siblings again. The same proportion (4%) thought they would not miss their siblings if they never saw them again.

Conclusions and implications for policy and practice

The development of residential care policy and practice and the understanding of the needs of individual children are largely informed by adult-centred assumptions and concerns. Information about children's relationships is often obtained from other adults, for example, parents, previous carers, social workers and teachers. The study suggests that children in middle childhood are capable of understanding family relationships and expressing their views on them. Children in residential care should be asked to define their own families and whom they regard as their siblings, rather than relying on adults' perceptions of the composition of the child's family.

Children's perceptions of the key characteristics of their relationships with their siblings indicate that they were able to recognise significant qualitative differences in their relationships with individual siblings. Siblings were liked and disliked for different reasons.

Children's preference for a particular sibling or siblings may have long-term consequences lasting throughout a lifetime. Studies of adults' kinship networks, reported by Finch (1989), suggest that a liking of a particular sibling is important for the siblings to maintain supportive contact in later life. It is vitally important for residential care workers to be aware of the quality of children's relationships with their individual siblings in order to enhance the development of supportive relationships with siblings lasting into adulthood.

An assessment of a child's sibling relationships, involving the child and as many of the siblings as possible and parents and previous carers, should be undertaken to ensure that a full and meaningful picture is obtained of the child's relationships with his or her siblings. A sibling relationship checklist, which is incorporated in the Department of Health (1991) research summary, offers a useful guide for assisting in the assessment of sibling relationships for children in residential care.

Separation from siblings was found to be a relatively common experience for the study children. It had a number of negative consequences for the children. Children missed their siblings even when separated for short periods of time. Children shared a number of joint friends with their siblings; however, joint friendships were only maintained when siblings lived together. Children who become separated from their siblings on entry to residential care also potentially lose part of their friendship network.

When comparing children's relationships with their siblings and friends, the study found that sibling relationships were characterised by greater emotional closeness, conflict, a sense of family identity and continuity of a relationship, in contrast to friends, who were perceived primarily in terms of companionship. Separation from siblings on entry or leaving residential care potentially disrupts the maintenance of emotional bonds and the development of family identity.

Siblings were perceived as a significant source of companionship, fun, support and help. Relationships with siblings appeared to be particularly important to the most isolated children, who had the smallest network of supportive relationships. Such children commonly enter residential care and may find it difficult to make friends at school or a residential unit. Maintenance of contact with siblings, especially older siblings, may be particularly important for such children.

Sibling conflict, fighting and domination by older siblings over their younger sisters and brothers appeared to be part of the sibling experience for the study children. Particular attention should be paid by residential workers to the negative side of the sibling dichotomy. Occasionally children may need protection from bullying and abuse by their siblings. However, sibling conflict on its own should not be a reason for separating siblings or discontinuing contact with separated siblings.

The long-term importance of siblings to children was demonstrated by the children's expectations of the future. They envisaged their siblings playing an important role in their lives in the future. Facilitating contact between children in residential care and their siblings, if a joint placement is not possible, is vitally important for the sake of the children's long-term welfare.

Contact between children and their siblings should take a variety of forms and be as natural as possible. Children should be allowed to spend time with their siblings without their parents' presence, unless for some good reason this is against the child's best interests. Perhaps a room could be made available in a residential unit, where children could receive visitors and play host, if the child's own room does not accommodate overnight visitors.

Nearly 90 per cent children in out-of-home placements eventually return to their families (Bullock, Little and Millham 1993). The return process can be equally as difficult for children as the original separation from home. Siblings can act as a bridge by assisting in the return process, particularly as children often return to a changed family situation. Siblings may be one of the few 'constants' in the rapidly changing families of children in residential care.

Finally, residential carers should view the children in their care in the wider context of their families, friendships and community networks. For many children links with their communities are frail or barely tenuous. For such children the knowledge of and contact with their separated siblings can act as an affirmation of family identity and sense of belonging.

Residential care workers may also assist the child by engaging in increased outreach work in the community with families of children in residential care. An increased involvement with the child's siblings may also benefit the staff, by assisting them in the greater understanding of the child and his or her needs. After all, who could possibly know you better than your sister or brother?

References

Bank, S. and Kahn, M.D. (1975) 'Sisterhood-brotherhood is powerful: Sibling sub-systems and family therapy.' *Family Process 14*, 311–337.

Bilson, A. and Barker, R. (1992/93) 'Siblings of children in care or accommodation: Neglected area of practice.' *Practice 6*, 4, 307–318.

Boer, F. (1990) *Sibling Relationships in Middle Childhood.* Leiden: Leiden DSWO Press.

Buchanan, A., Wheal, A., Walder, D., MacDonald, S. and Coker, R. (1993) *Answering Back – Report by Young People being Looked After on The Children Act 1989.* Southampton: University of Southampton.

Buhrmester, D. and Furman, W. (1990) 'Perceptions of sibling relationships during middle childhood and adolescence.' *Child Development 61*, 1387–1398.

Bullock, R., Little, M. and Millham, S. (1993) *Going Home – The Return of Children Separated from Their Families.* Aldershot: Dartmouth.

Cicirelli, V.G. (1982) 'Sibling influence throughout the life span.' In M.E. Lamb and B. Sutton-Smith (eds) *Sibling Relationships: Their Nature and Significance Across the Life Span.* Hillsdale, New Jersey: Lawrence Erlbaum Associates.

Department of Health (1991) *Patterns and Outcomes in Child Placement, Messages from Current Research and Their Implications.* London: HMSO.

Dunn, J. and McGuire, S. (1992) 'Sibling and peer relationships in childhood.' *Journal of Child Psychology and Psychiatry 33*, 1, 67–105.

Farmer, E. and Parker, R. (1991) *Trials and Tribulations: Returning Children from Local Authority Care to their Families.* London: HMSO.

Finch, J. (1989) *Family Obligations and Social Change.* Cambridge: Polity Press.

Fletcher, B. (1993) *Not Just a Name – The Views of Young People in Foster and Residential Care.* London: National Consumer Council.

Furman, W. (1990) *Sibling Relationship Questionnaire – Revised (Child) 3/90*, Denver: Department of Psychology, University of Denver.

Furman, W. and Buhrmester, D. (1985) 'Children's perceptions of the personal relationships in their social networks.' *Developmental Psychology 21*, 6, 1016–1024.

Kosonen, M. (1994) 'Sibling relationships for children in the care system.' *Adoption and Fostering 18*, 3, 30–35.

Kosonen, M. (1996a) Maintaining sibling relationships: neglected dimension in child care practice. *British Journal of Social Work 26*, 809–822.

Kosonen, M. (1996b) 'Siblings as providers of support and care during middle childhood: Children's perceptions.' *Children and Society 10*, 267–279.

McAuley, C. (1996) *Children in Long-term Foster Care: Emotional and Social Development.* Aldershot: Avebury.

MacLean, K. (1991) 'Meeting the needs of sibling groups in care.' *Adoption and Fostering 15*, 1, 33–37.

Millham, S., Bullock, R., Hosie, K. and Haak, M. (1986) *Lost in Care: The Problem of Maintaining Links Between Children in Care and their Families.* Aldershot: Gower.

Morgan, D.H. (1980) 'The social definition of the family.' In M. Anderson (ed) *Sociology of the Family.* Harmondsworth: Penguin.

Rowe, J., Cain, H., Hundleby, M. and Keane, A. (1984) *Long-term Foster Care.* London: Batsworth.

Simpson, B. (1994) 'Bringing the "unclear" family into focus: Divorce and re-marriage in contemporary Britain.' *Man (N.S.) 29*, 831–851.

Stein, M. and Carey, K. (1986) *Leaving Care.* Oxford: Basil Blackwell.

Thorpe, R. (1980) 'The experience of children and parents living apart: Implications and guidelines for practice.' In J. Triseliotis (ed) *New Developments in Foster Care and Adoption.* London: Routledge and Kegan Paul.

Treffers, P.D.A., Goedhart, A.V., Waltz, J.W. and Kouldijs, P. (1990) 'The systematic collection of patient data in a centre for child and adolescent psychiatry.' *British Journal of Psychiatry 157*, 744–748.

Wedge, P. and Mantle, G. (1991) *Sibling Groups and Social Work: A Study of Children Referred for Permanent Substitute Family Placement.* Aldershot: Avebury.

Weinstein, E.A. (1960) *The Self Image of the Foster Child.* New York: Russell Sage Foundation.

Whitaker, D.S., Cook, J.M., Dunn, C. and Rockliffe, S. (1984) *The Experience of Residential Care from the Perspective of Children, Parents and Caregivers.* Report to ESRC, University of York.

CHAPTER 10

Peer Groups:
A Neglected Resource

John Hudson

Peer groups have played a central role in child development for generations. But, since the early part of the twentieth century, their significance in child development has been ignored in much of the English-speaking world and their influence generally regarded as negative rather than positive. There was virtually no research on peer groups between 1930 and 1970 (Lewis and Rosenblum 1975) while interest in the social sciences focused on vertical relationships such as mother–child and manager–worker rather than child–child or worker–worker.

Yet relationships with peers have a significant impact on children's opportunities for development: before school, in primary school, secondary school and higher education and at work and leisure. Children who lack early experience of peer interaction, or who experience low levels of social interaction, often demonstrate deficits in social competence that restrict their ability to make satisfying relationships with their peers later in life. By contrast, in some cases access to supportive peer relationships can help children to negotiate adverse family situations.

As peer group research is a relatively recent phenomenon, there are many gaps and apparent inconsistencies in the findings to date (Dunn and McGuire 1992) but there is enough evidence to provide a framework for understanding the potential significance of peer relationships for child development and to point to likely future areas for research.

In this chapter I will first set out some of the themes which have arisen in research on peer relationships as they develop through childhood and adolescence. These have mostly been based on observations of children in formal institutions like nurseries and school where interaction is largely with people of very similar age. Interaction with 'peers' in a wider sense, including those a few years older or younger, may be different as illustrated by sibling relationships and social play away from school (Hill and Tisdall 1997).

I will then consider some of the approaches to group care which have drawn on peer interaction. I will argue that, while these approaches have drawn on peer interaction to promote certain aspects of development and/or rehabilitation, understanding of peer interactions has other contributions to make. Finally, I will argue for a radical rethink of residential child care in the UK because current practices are detrimental to children's development and undermine their chances of recovery following bad experiences.

Peer interaction in the early years

Children are able to interact with peers by at least the age of 10 months – or at about the time they begin to lose their fear of strangers generally. Some children appear to do so even earlier. During their second year they show a preference for peers over strange adults but, around the age of 20 months, a fear of strange peers develops which seems to echo the earlier generalised fear of strangers. This goes by the middle of the third year, prompting Kagan, Kearsley and Zelago (1975) to argue that this represents a stage in cognitive development (similar perhaps to the ability to see danger).

Observation in group settings indicates that during the first two years of life visual interaction and signalling is more frequent than shared play with toys (Bronson 1975), though large immovable toys encourage positive interaction among young children (Vandell and Mueller 1980). In other words, infants are interested in what each other does, but cooperative behaviour develops slowly. Children gradually acquire a repertoire of behaviours for use with different children; for example, they are more likely to imitate older peers.

Those who experience high quality care outside the family gain from it while those, such as first-born or only children, who experience fewer opportunities for peer interaction or who experience exclusively maternal care, tend to have a smaller repertoire of skills and are more likely to have difficulties with their peers (Howes 1990). By the age of five 'socially competent' children tend to be positive, helpful and supportive in their relationships with other children and these characteristics continue to form the basis for popularity among older children.

Peer interaction in primary school

Primary (or elementary) school sees a new stage in the development of friendships while gender separation becomes more pronounced. Gender identity is usually stable by the age of four and is consolidated over the primary school period when children show greatest aversion to spending much time with members of the opposite sex (Goldman and Goldman 1982). Indeed, during this period, gender is more important than race in influencing interaction acceptance (Carter, Detine-Carter and Forrest 1980; Sluckin 1981).

Lee (1973) showed that even among infants in their first year, preferences are apparent which lead to popularity or unpopularity. However, by primary (or elementary) school, a number of clearly distinguishable characteristics have emerged which tend to be associated with peer acceptance or rejection (Asher and Corie 1991; Bee 1992) (Figure 10.1).

In the longer term, rejected children are more likely to drop out of school, though a significant minority of rejected children do remain in school. Peer rejection tends to be associated with parent–child difficulties (Rutter and Rutter 1993).

Popular children are more likely to be:

- Friendly towards others, less punitive, more reinforcing, more supportive
- Outgoing and gregarious
- Physically attractive
- Physically larger or taller or more mature
- The youngest child in the family
- Good at specific task skills, such as sports or games
- More successful in school.

Rejected children are more likely to be:

- Physically unattractive
- Physically or emotionally immature
- Aggressive or disruptive
- Less friendly, critical rather than supportive.

Figure 10.1 Some characteristics of popular and rejected children in primary (elementary) school

Peers and play

As noted earlier, play with toys forms a very small part of the interaction between young infants who often play alongside each other rather than together. In addition, the more socially skilled infants are, the less they rely on toys to maintain interaction with other infants (Vandell and Mueller 1980).

As children develop cognitively, their ability to introduce fantasy and make-believe into their play also develops. Much primary school play – and toy marketing – is based on children's capacity for fantasy and make-believe (Cohen 1993).

Play is stimulated by novel but similar experiences and by the opportunity to move on to more complex tasks once simpler ones have been accomplished.

Towards the end of the primary school period, increasing sex segregation in play activities leads to a stage where the ways in which children manage their play begins to differ. Boys continue to value physical games and will appeal to the rules in any dispute whereas girls begin to explore the relationships that are sustained through play and will suspend an activity in order to sort out a relationship difficulty (Gilligan 1982). Girls tend to develop play with two or three others, whereas boys often prefer larger groups (Erwin 1993; Hartup 1992).

Peers and friendship

Bigelow and La Gaipa (1980) argue that friendship does not fully emerge until the teens. However, infants react more positively to known than unknown peers, while primary school children select play companions on the basis of at least some interpersonal characteristics. Opportunity plays a large part in determining the range of available friends; for example, children in a formal classroom are less likely to develop as wide a range of friendships as children in an open classroom where they are able to interact with more children (Miller and Gentry 1980).

During primary (or elementary) school, children have friendships largely based on common activities and often not with age mates but with those slightly older or younger than them. This may offer a basis for the admiration which is often found as part of a developing friendship. Popular children are more likely to have longer relationships with similarly popular children. Gradually, choices based on interests and personality become more important influences on friendships (Hartup 1992).

Some children, however, appear to become 'rejected children' fairly early on. Initially, this does not appear to restrict the range of their relationships but, by the late primary stage, these children are less likely to be able to make relationships with 'popular' children and may then form groups of their own (Asher and Corie 1991). Up to one-quarter of children are victims of bullying, though fewer children regularly bully others. The incidence of bullying is much affected by the ways adults promote cooperation and control aggression (Smith and Sharp 1994).

From the early teens, the idea of permanence in relationships begins to emerge but developmental progress has often put distance between children who were developmentally closer in primary school. Combined with changes of school, this leads on to the selection of new friends. On average, the move towards stable relationships is faster for girls than boys throughout their teens so that, for example, by their mid-teens girls typically place much greater value on issues like loyalty and commitment than do boys (Bigelow and La Gaipa 1980). Of course there are exceptions to these generalisations.

Indeed, a focus on feelings and cooperation rather than on doing and dominance generally separates girls and boys from the late primary through to the early secondary school years (Archer 1992). While more boys choose friends on the basis of activities rather than feelings until the mid-teens, more girls choose friends, including friends of the opposite sex, on the basis of feelings from the later primary school period onwards. Many boys only begin to explore emotions in their mid-teens, sometimes in tandem with growing intimacy with girls (Goldman and Goldman 1982).

Peer interaction in adolescence

Popular traditional notions of adolescence as a period of peer pressure and 'storm and stress' have given way in the past three decades to the realisation that most adolescents have fairly equanimous relationships with their parents and peers (Douvan and Adelson 1966; Fogelman 1976; Rutter et al. 1976). They often choose peers whose values are in tune with their parents' values (Youniss and Smollar 1985) and manage to deal with the transition to adulthood relatively successfully (Coleman and Hendry 1990).

The notion of peer pressure in adolescence may represent an over-generalisation of the final stages of sex-segregated peer groups which was prominent in primary school. Compliance with group norms appears to be at its greatest but this is almost a prelude to the breakup of these groups as adolescents begin to form larger, mixed-sex groups which are the forum for the exploration of sexual relationships (Dunphy 1969). Though some friendships may remain throughout this period, the composition of the groups of which an adolescent is a member will usually evolve over this period. This seems entirely reasonable in the light of findings that peers satisfy differing but complementary needs for adolescents compared with parents and other adults (Youniss and Smollar 1985).

Gender and ethnic identity

The primary school years see the consolidation of gender identity in the sense that girls and boys identify themselves as female and male respectively and usually mix with others of the same sex (Goldman and Goldman 1982). During the late primary and early secondary school years girls and boys increasingly operate in sex-segregated groups where they develop many gender-specific norms (Archer 1992). Then in their mid-teens, they begin to develop a sense of sexual identity. At this stage one in twenty or more may express a preference for being of the opposite sex (Goldman and Goldman 1982). Up to one in ten adolescents may express a preference for homosexual relationships.

Children from majority ethnic groups follow a similar pattern in reaching a sense of ethnic identity, expressing greatest preference for their own ethnic group in the primary school years and less so in their teens; children from minority ethnic groups are more likely to express a preference for the majority group in their primary school years and for their own group in their teens (Vaughan 1987). This can be seen as a response to racist images and models favouring the white majority, which black and ethnic minority children gradually overcome (Robinson 1995).

Ethnic minority children and those of mixed parentage usually learn to operate differently in interaction with black or white peers (Wilson 1987). Similarly, Heller (1987) reports that some Québequois develop bilingualism and an ability to function satisfactorily in two cultures without being part of both. This is often expressed in linguistic jokes which demonstrate the bilinguals' competence in both languages, but many use one language with adults and the other with their peers.

Conclusions about peer development

By the mid-teens most adolescents will have a sense of their gender, sexual and ethnic identities and of the norms appropriate to those identities. The development of identity and adaptations such as bilingualism all depend in part on opportunities for peer interaction in infancy, in primary school, in their sex-segregated groups around the period of transition from primary to secondary school and in the mixed-sex groups of mid-adolescence.

Access to friendship and positive peer relations enhances the amount of interaction children have, the amount of information they receive about the world, their experience of relationships and their social skills (Hartup 1992).

Though Hartup does not believe that friendships are essential to development, only an advantage, it is difficult to see how children can gain an adequate sense of their gender, sexual and ethnic identity without such relationships.

The comparative significance of adult caregivers

In stressing the significance of peers in child development, it is crucial not to underestimate the importance of adult caregivers. For many children, the initial confidence to interact with others comes from a secure relationship with one or more caregivers, usually their parent. However, for some children, a sibling relationship or a relationship with a peer may become an important source of stability, particularly if the adults in their lives are unable to offer that stability.

The development of formal language skills is particularly stimulated by adults because children will use more complex language with adults than with other children. Children who converse solely with other children or with adults who do not extend their use of language tend to be deficient in linguistic skills. This suggests one reason why poor quality day and institutional care have such poor outcomes compared with high quality day and institutional care (Scarr and Dunn 1987).

As with language skills, adult interaction seems to stimulate cognitive development. Parental support, for example, particularly of fathers to their daughters, has a positive effect on academic attainment, as does good teaching. In adolescence, parents continue to have considerable influence on issues such as achievement, occupation and education and to be regarded as an important source of nurturance (Coleman 1974) which for some young people may last well into adulthood.

Up to the early teens, mothers and fathers usually remain the main providers of emotional support to children, though peers can be important for certain kinds of confidences (Furman and Buhrmester 1985). But the ways in which children draw on adult and peer interaction will depend on the situations in which they find themselves. Labov (1970), for example, found that children from minority ethnic groups who were inhibited in their use of language when talking to adults from the majority group, because they could not use the more complex language of the majority group, would speak more freely in the presence of a peer with whom they felt more relaxed without the pressure to conform to adult expectations.

Consequences of lack of peer interaction

Those who, as infants, lack experience of peers will probably be less socially competent at the age of four. During primary (or elementary) school, they will be less likely to be selected for friendships by peers. In the late primary/early secondary years, they will be more likely to have been marginalised in (or excluded from) sex-segregated groups and thus restricted in the choice of same-sex peers with whom to develop friendships.

Such situations can have other consequences. Children who are being abused and who lack peer interaction may have less opportunity to find out that their abuse is not normal or to seek support from others to deal with their abuse.

Girls who have not experienced sex-segregated groups and learned the importance of acceptance, loyalty and commitment may find they are rejected by their peers because they do not understand the norms of their gender.

The use of peer interaction in alternative care

In one sense, peer groups have a long history in UK child care. When the Philanthropic Society set up its children's homes in the 1790s in which children were cared for as 'apprentices' in the 'master's' house, they were creating the opportunities for peer interaction which 'normal' apprentices would have had. Most nineteenth century children's provision in the UK worked because the peer groups made them work – there simply were not sufficient staff for 'individual' care. Subsequently, although peer interactions almost by default played an important part in group care, the explicit use of peer interactions has been confined to a few aspects of child development.

However, the early twentieth century saw three interesting articulations of the positive role of peer groups in caring for children in need – Father Flanagan's 'Boys' Town' in Nebraska, Homer Lane's 'Little Commonwealth' in England and Anton Makarenko's home in Russia. Both Father Flanagan and Makarenko (1984) were trying to put into practice 'revolutionary' ideas of promoting more flexible and democratic approaches to care of the groups of children. These were also reflected in the practice of the Scottish anarchist A.S. Neill (1985) and the 'Shared Responsibility' movement (Beedell 1995). They sought to keep similar 'revolutionary' ideas alive when the 'mainstream' of social work in the UK was taken over by psychodynamic and, later, social learning approaches to child care.

Both the psychodynamic and the social learning schools rely heavily on adult intervention in children's lives; the content of therapy focuses on feelings or behaviour respectively and the outcomes on issues such as confidence and individual behaviour. Even when a group approach is used, the emphasis is on the therapist/behaviourist managing the group rather than on the contribution of the young people (Redl and Wineman 1952, 1967; Ayllon and Arzin 1968; Konopka 1972; Brown and Christie 1981). Whereas those approaches have seen group care as a 'setting' within which to practise treatment, much as a hospital is a setting for medical interventions, others like Winnicott and Britton (1957) argued cogently for the healing function of peer relations within group care.

The idea that those in need of help can at the same time help others was most clearly articulated in the work of the psychiatrist Maxwell Jones, who pioneered the 'therapeutic community' for adults in Scotland. The idea that group care can be therapeutic was not new – Mary Carpenter, Pestalozzi, Homer Lane, Rainer and others had all suggested its potential for therapy. Winnicott and Britton (1957) had described the 'therapeutic' use of group care for evacuees during the Second World War. But Maxwell Jones appears to have been the first to emphasise the therapeutic use of peer interaction. Many children's establishments now call themselves 'therapeutic communities', but only a few closely follow Jones' principles by involving peers in treating each other. This involves enabling children and young people to learn to make their own decisions while respecting the views and rights of others.

Wolins (1974), researching child care in Israel and Europe, outlined a cognitive basis for these more democratic forms of residential care, concluding that peer group support is a key factor in successful child care. Wolins drew on work by Kohlberg which has since been rightly criticised by Gilligan (1982) for being sexist, but Kohlberg's suggestion that there is a stage in moral development characterised by adherence to peer group norms is reflected in the findings about compliance in sex-segregated groups. The implication was that residential staff should work with and not against the grain of groups. This involves negotiating shared responsibility between staff and residents.

Wolins (1973) also argued that children at different ages need appropriate kinds of residential environments reflecting their cognitive development from infancy when they are entirely dependent on adults, to maturity when they are able to enter into full mutual 'exchange'. As this chapter has shown, this is based on too simplistic a model of child development, since children engage in peer interaction from infancy and parents continue to nurture their children well into adulthood. However, as Anthony (1973), Goldman and Goldman (1982) and Gilligan (1982), among others, show, there are significant shifts in the ways children think about the world as they grow older and this applies as much to their peer interactions as to other aspects of their lives.

I first came across 'Shared Responsibility' in the late 1960s at a girls' hostel in Oxford (Critchley and Fann 1971a and b; Hague 1976) where, interestingly, Arnold Critchley, like Makarenko, appears to have developed it out of dialogue with the young people. When I subsequently tried to adapt the principles to Bunbury House in Ellesmere Port (Morton 1979), I found, at the outset, that the young people initially wanted strict compliance with the group's rules but, as they and the group developed, they became more flexible, moving from what Wolins calls 'nomocracy' towards 'other-orientation'.

Implications for residential care

The findings reviewed so far in this chapter highlight the need to understand and work with the potential of peer group relations to act as resources for learning, stimulation and support, as well as to reject, bully and stereotype. A number of implications arise for the management of residential homes and schools. First, all alternative care placements should be based on the assumption that they will facilitate *both* family contact *and* peer interaction in the child's development. It is interesting to explore how in the novel *Anne of Green Gables*, written around the time that Father Flanagan, Homer Lane and Anton Makarenko were at work, the eponymous heroine becomes accepted in the community through a combination of adult and peer group acceptance and through her educational success. For children in residential care it is as important to sustain previous friendships as to encourage positive relationships with current co-residents (Triseliotis *et al.* 1995).

Second, a care career entailing multiple placements combined with significant resident and staff turnover as practised in the UK is likely to be extremely damaging. I suggest that a major factor in the destructiveness of multiple placements, apart from the inevitable loss and anger engendered by the many moves, is the disruption to peer relationships. The time needed to develop the common ground for and the commitment to a new relationship (Hartup 1992) is simply not available to a child subject to frequent moves.

Third, the increasingly high rate of school exclusions in the UK is likely to be damaging not only to children's intellectual development but also to their social and emotional development as they miss out on normal peer group developmental experiences. The use of school exclusion is particularly ironic when we know that 'rejected children' are more likely to drop out of school anyway. School absence, whether as a result of exclusion, refusal or other form of non-attendance, is a major problem in British children's homes (Berridge and Brodie 1998).

Fourth, putting lots of children without stable peer relationships into (increasingly small) children's homes is a recipe for disaster since they are more likely to form 'anti-social' peer relationships if they have no experience of 'pro-social' peer relationships. It is not without significance, in my view, that Triseliotis et al. (1995) found that children in residential schools did better than many children placed in children's homes or foster homes. The schools have a greater chance to develop a (relatively) stable peer group than many small establishments and they also, one suspects, provide an image of continuity which is increasingly absent from other agency interventions in the UK!

Group care has increasingly been used for children who have been neglected or damaged during the course of their upbringing (Department of Health 1998). The emphasis on adult intervention at the expense of peer interaction has affected both the ways children's normal developmental needs have been addressed and the ways in which 'rehabilitation' has been provided. Staffing has been increased but much less so staff training, on the assumption that sheer numbers of adults will be able to provide for all a child's developmental needs, when we know that many of these are provided by peers. While higher numbers of adults may enable more personalised care to be provided for the rehabilitation of some children, it is by no means clear that all forms of rehabilitation are dependent on adult interventions (or that those that are can always be successfully carried out by untrained staff!).

Several possible areas in which peer interaction can contribute to 'rehabilitation' seem worth exploring, particularly in view of our knowledge of normal child development. Group care can bring children into contact with peers whatever their age or need. At least some offending and 'anti-social' behaviour arises from lack of peer group skills. Extending the range and scope of children's peer interactions can enable them to recover lost developmental experience and, hopefully, restore to them the advantages of positive peer group experiences. This is particularly true of children who by reason of disability or abuse and neglect have been cut off from peer interactions.

Peers can often provide more appropriate support and interventions because cognitively they are closer to the child and can speak their language. Children's understanding of death and loss (Anthony 1973) and of sexual behaviour (Goldman and Goldman 1982) develops throughout their childhood and, while adults have a role to play in offering support and providing explanations, other children's closer cognitive and sometimes emotional development can also provide helpful ways of relating to and sharing that experience. Interestingly, recent approaches to dealing with bullying in school – which itself can be an indication of poor peer group skills – have used peers both to address the issue and to provide support to victims (Smith and Sharp 1994).

Peers can be important in motivating for change. We are less likely to be inspired or influenced by distant adult ideals than by models of behaviour which are slightly ahead of us. For many children and young people, slightly more mature peers may be better motivators for change than any number of skilled adults. This does not mean that there is no place for adults but that their skills should be used to maximise the support young people give each other and to increase the influence of more mature young people. It will often be easier for others of similar age to reach children as they are emotionally and cognitively closer than staff – a fact recognised by the most skilled child care workers.

Finally, peers can bring genuine healing both consciously and unconsciously to those who have suffered hurt. I have observed this on a number of occasions in group care and it is worth noting that, when Harlow sought to 'cure' the monkeys whom he had 'disturbed' by depriving them of their mothers, his eventual 'solution' was not 'a good mother' but 'a good peer group' (Novak and Harlow 1975).

Conclusion

The continuing concentration on 'individual' approaches to child care in the UK ignores the importance of peer interactions in a child's development towards 'an individual life in society' (Preamble to the UN Convention on the Rights of the Child 1989). Much of the damage and distress caused by the child care system in the UK can be traced to this emphasis, to the scope it has given for abusers to clothe their abuse in 'individual therapy' and to the increasingly desperate search for placements in which an 'ideal' adult will meet a child's needs, forgetting that much of a child's developmental needs are met through peer interaction.

Much of the stress placed on child care staff can also be linked to the assumption that they, as adults, must be the 'carers', rather than the facilitators of care by others, including the peer group. Improved staffing ratios will not resolve the problems in British residential child care, unless carers are trained in the complexities of child development and shown how to use the positive resources that peer interactions can bring.

References

Anthony, S. (1973) *The Discovery of Death in Childhood and After.* Harmondsworth: Penguin.

Archer, J. (1992) 'Childhood gender roles: Social context and organisation.' In H. McGurk (ed) *Childhood Social Development.* Hove: Laurence Erlbaum.

Ayllon, T. and Arzin, N. (1968) *The Token Economy.* New York: Appleton-Century-Crofts.

Asher, S.R. and Corie, J.D. (eds) (1991) *Peer Rejection in Childhood.* Cambridge: Cambridge University Press.

Bee, H. (1992) *The Developing Child,* 6th edition. New York: Harper Collins College Publishers.

Beedell, C. (1995) 'Sharing power and responsibility.' *Therapeutic Care and Education 4,* 3, 3–11.

Berridge, D. and Brodie, I. (1998) *Children's Homes Revisited.* London: Jessica Kingsley Publishers.

Bigelow, B.J. and La Gaipa, J.J. (1980) 'The development of friendship values and choice.' In H.C. Foot, A.J. Chapman and J.R. Smith (eds) *Friendship and Social Relations in Children.* Chichester: Wiley.

Bronson, W.C. (1975) 'Developments in behaviour with age mates during the second year of life.' In M. Lewis and L.A. Rosenblum (eds) *Friendship and Peer Relations.* Chichester: Wiley.

Brown, B.J. and Christie, M. (1981) *Social Learning Practice in Residential Child Care.* Oxford: Pergamon.

Carter, D.E., Detine-Carter, S.L. and Forrest, W. (1980) 'Interracial acceptance in the classroom.' In H.C. Foot, A.J. Chapman and J.R. Smith (eds) *Friendship and Social Relations in Children.* Chichester: Wiley.

Cohen, D. (1993) *The Development of Play.* London: Routledge.

Coleman, J.C. (1974) *Relations in Adolescence.* London: Routledge & Kegan Paul.

Coleman, J.C. and Hendry, L.B. (1990) *The Nature of Adolescence.* London: Routledge.

Critchley, A. and Fann, B. (1971a) 'Group work with adolescent girls – Part I: Setting up the group.' *Child in Care 11,* 5, 17–23.

Critchley, A. and Fann, B. (1971b) 'Group work with adolescent girls – Part II: A lost opportunity.' *Child in Care 11,* 6, 11–14.

Department of Health (1998) *Caring for Children Away from Home.* Chichester: Wiley.

Douvan. E. and Adelson, J. (1966) *The Adolescent Experience.* Chichester: Wiley.

Dunn, J. and McGuire, S. (1992) 'Sibling and peer relationships in childhood.' *Journal of Child Psychology and Psychiatry 33,* 1, 67–105.

Dunphy, D.C. (1969) *Cliques, Crowds and Gangs.* Australia: Cheshire.

Ellis, M.J. and Scholtz, G.J.L. (1978) *Activity and Play of Children.* New York: Prentice Hall.

Erwin, P. (1993) *Friendship and Peer Relations in Children.* Chichester: Wiley.

Fogelman, K. (1976) *Britain's Sixteen Year Olds.* London: National Children's Bureau.

Furman, W. and Buhrmester, D. (1985) 'Children's perceptions of the personal relationship in their social networks.' *Developmental Psychology 21,* 6, 1016–1024.

Gilligan, C. (1982) *In a Different Voice.* London: Harvard University Press.

Goldman, R. and Goldman, J. (1982) *Children's Sexual Thinking.* London: Routledge and Kegan Paul.

Hague, G. (1976) 'Struggling to build a shared responsibility system.' *Residential Social Work 16,* 8, 207–212.

Hartup, W.W. (1992) 'Friendships and their developmental significance.' In H. McGurk (ed) *Childhood Social Development.* Hove: Laurence Erlbaum.

Heller, M. (1987) 'The role of language in the formation of ethnic identity.' In J.S. Phinney and M.J. Rotheram (eds) *Children's Ethnic Socialisation.* London: Sage.

Hill, M. and Tisdall, K. (1997) *Children and Society.* Harlow: Longman.

Howes, C. (1990) 'Can the age of entry into child care and the quality of child care predict adjustment into kindergarten?' *Developmental Psychology 26,* 292–303.

Kagan, J., Kearsley, R.B. and Zelago, P.R. (1975) 'The emergence of initial apprehension to unfamiliar peers.' In M. Lewis and L.A. Rosenblumm (eds) *Friendship and Peer Relations.* Chichester: Wiley.

Konopka, G. (1972) *Social Group Work: A Helping Process,* 2nd Edition. London: Prentice Hall.

Labov, W. (1970) 'The logic of non-standard English.' In F. William (ed) *Language and Poverty.* Chicago: Markham.

Lee, L.C. (1973) 'Social encounters of infants: The beginnings of popularity.' Cited in Hartup (1975).

Lewis, M. and Rosenblum, L.A. (eds) (1975) *Friendship and Peer Relations.* Chichester: Wiley.

Makarenko, A. (1984) *The Road to Life.* London: Central Books.

Miller, N. and Gentry, K.W. (1980) 'Sociometric indices of children's peer interaction in the school setting.' In H.C. Foot, A.J. Chapman and J.R. Smith (eds) *Friendship and Social Relations in Children.* Chichester: Wiley.

Morton, S. (1979) 'Adolescents in care: An inside view.' *Social Work Today 10,* 28, 32.

Neill, A.S. (1985) *Summerhill.* Harmondsworth: Penguin.

Novak, M. and Harlow, H. (1975) 'Social recovery of monkeys isolated for the first years of life.' *Developmental Psychology 11,* 453–465.

Redl, F. and Wineman, D. (1952) *Control from Within.* New York: Free Press.

Redl, F. and Wineman, D. (1967) *Children Who Hate*, 2nd Edition. New York: Free Press.

Robinson, L. (1995) *Psychology for Social Workers: Black Perspectives.*

Rutter, M., Graham, P., Chadwick, O. and Yule, W. (1976) 'Adolescent turmoil: Fact or fiction?' *Journal of Child Psychology and Psychiatry 17*, 35–56.

Rutter, M. and Rutter, M. (1993) *Developing Minds.* Harmondsworth: Penguin.

Scarr, S. and Dunn, J. (1987) *Mother Care/Other Care.* Harmondsworth: Penguin.

Sluckin, A. (1981) *Growing up in the Playground.* London: RKP.

Smith, P.K. and Sharp, S. (eds) (1994) *School Bullying.* London: Routledge.

Triseliotis, J., Borland, M., Hill, M. and Lambert, L. (1995) *Teenagers and the Social Work Services.* London: HMSO.

Vandell, D.L. and Mueller, E.C. (1980) 'Peer play and friendships during the first two years.' In H.C. Foot, A.J. Chapman and J.R. Smith (eds) *Friendship and Social Relations in Children.* Chichester: Wiley.

Vaughan, G.M. (1987) 'A social psychological model of ethnic identity development.' In J.S. Phinney and M.J. Rotheram (eds) *Children's Ethnic Socialisation.* London: Sage.

Wilson, A. (1987) *Mixed Race Children.* London: Allen and Urwin.

Winnicott, D.W. and Britton, C. (1957) 'Residential management as treatment for difficult children.' In D.W. Winnicott (ed) *The Child and the Outside World.* London: Tavistock.

Wolins, M. (1973) 'Some theoretical observations on group care.' In D.M. Pappenfort, D.M. Kilpatrick and R.W. Roberts (eds) *Child Caring: Social Policy and the Institution.* Chicago: Aldine.

Wolins, M. (ed) (1974) *Successful Group Care.* Chicago: Aldine.

Youniss, J. and Smollar, J. (1985) *Adolescent Relations with Mothers, Fathers and Friends.* Chicago: Chicago University Press.

CHAPTER 11

Conclusion: Perspectives in Residential Child Care

Mono Chakrabarti

Introduction

The contributors to this book have examined an extensive range of substantive, theoretical, methodological and operational policy-related issues which have implications for future research and development of service provisions relating to children and young people who are being looked after. In this final section, the aim is to explore some of the main themes which appeared in preceding chapters, and to draw out salient issues. This book is intended to make available information from research, management and practice about new developments in residential child care designed to promote children's family and network relationships. Drawing on material from several countries around the world, the book has attempted to explore both systems in general and particular projects which aim to involve families and other network members in the planning and care of children looked after in residential units or children's homes.

This concluding chapter will also introduce the debate around the significance of social exclusion in relation to children and young people and their families from minority ethnic backgrounds. It is now widely acknowledged that social discrimination is often a source of profound disadvantage for a number of groups and individuals worldwide. First, however, it is important to look briefly at the notion of 'welfare state' at the turn of this century and its impact on individuals and families.

Social welfare state

The idea of welfare is a complex concept to unravel. As Titmuss (1979) has noted, concepts of welfare can imply very different things to different people and different models of public welfare assume different forms and contain different assumptions about means and ends.

This statement suggests a more useful approach to the analysis of social welfare than confining it, as still too often occurs, within certain simple assumptions. One such is that welfare is the progressive compensation for the costs of economic growth. Another is that it is a capitalist ploy for its own preservation and a third is that it is an altruistic activity based on humanitarian values. It may in fact be any or all of these and many other things besides.

Individualisation in Western countries has been associated with a number of fundamental social changes; two of which are the rate at which the age structure of the population has changed and the concentration of that population in urban areas. The institutions of the social welfare state emerged as a response to these new pressures and to the need for the quality and quantity of the labour force to be maintained and enhanced. Everywhere the central purpose remains as Ford and Chakrabarti (1988) suggest: to compensate for loss of income resulting from temporary or permanent incapacity; to provide an income for those who are retired or who are permanently incapacitated from earning an income; to provide health care, directly or indirectly; to provide education; and to make available personal social services for those whose welfare requires professional intervention.

Much analysis of industrial society has tended to emphasise the development of the liberal democratic state in Western countries and to suggest that the rights of citizens have become an important focus. From this perspective, the welfare state has been closely associated with the definition and extension of citizenship rights. Not only were new social services gradually introduced to cover all sections of the population but the evolution of those services has been linked with the extension of the political franchise.

In exploring alternative methods of social welfare provision, a number of questions need to be considered. First, one might question the validity of the apparently simple equation made by many people that welfare state is synonymous with the availability of welfare. Second, one might challenge the extent to which the institutions of the welfare state in developed countries have promoted equality within the population for which they provide, or whether indeed this is a legitimate function.

The debate continues as this millennium comes to an end. 'Globalisation' gives a further twist to the complex process through which 'social, economic and technological changes [arise from] the dismantling of national and regional barriers to trade and communication ...' (Trevillion 1997). As these changes have encompassed the advanced countries, two particular dangers have become evident. First, technological developments have allowed capital to flow readily in the direction of a most favourable return, sometimes resulting in investment in the economies of the developing world at the expense of the advanced economies; the economic dislocation has placed considerable pressure on funding of the welfare state. Second, globalisation has resulted in the wide dissemination of an inherently conservative, American ideology which generally regards collective and essentially government intervention in welfare with great suspicion (Cadman and Chakrabarti 1999).

Increasing diversity in families

The changing nature of family sizes, structure, functions and roles in developed countries represents an area of potential concern for children's welfare. Global economic changes have tended to generate convergence towards families in which children grow up in significantly smaller units, normally where both parents are working and, in a growing number of cases, in households where only one of the adults may be their birth parents. Many children also experience periods of life in lone-parent households.

The benefits of dual parent income may not always compensate for the absence of effective and affordable child care or, indeed, as is particularly evident in the USA, for the lack of guaranteed maternity allowance and paid parental leave. The continuing, apparently irreversible, trend towards lone parenthood certainly increases the prospect of impoverishment for a growing proportion of children throughout our varied economies. There is little evidence that many of these countries have given active thought to the enormity of the changes needed to provide support to children and their families in their very changed circumstances and needs (Rampakash 1994).

The book and issues addressed

Malcolm Hill in the first two introductory chapters reviewed briefly developments in residential child care towards a more open, network-based approach and away from notions of closed or inward-looking institutions. The chapters provide a framework for assessment and intervention, which take account of individual needs, internal group dynamics within the establishments and children's wider social network relationships. He then focuses on the nature and complexity of contact between children in care in an institutional environment and their families and the role of professionals in facilitating the links with families. Theoretical issues in relation to residential child care and the place of families in it are further examined, highlighting the need to adopt a more inclusive and flexible orientation.

Chapter 3 by Turnbull identifies children's needs as a basis for a total system of services, including residential child care, within a local area. An example is described from an area where a decentralised structure was established with the aim of producing flexibility of services and readier moves between different elements of the system. A vital ingredient of service development has been networking between residential staff and other professionals and agencies.

Fariss in Chapter 4 outlines the role of a large voluntary organisation with a seventy-five year history in residential care, which has contracted an important role with statutory child protection services. The agency offers a specialist service, focusing on placement prevention, but with a residential component mainly to provide respite in crises. The programme involves intensive help and support to children and their families on a planned basis with built-in follow-up and outreach services.

In the following Chapter 5 Halliday collates the finding of in-depth interviews with parents, young people and staff concerning collaboration within a residential child care agency. The study provides insight into the factors which promote cooperation and enables families with major personal difficulties to work together effectively with a view to finding a resolution to some of the inevitable tensions.

Ridgely argues in Chapter 6 that residential treatment could be designed in a manner which strengthens family competence to function more effectively. She suggests that residential staff would need to alter their ways of thinking to work with the family as a whole rather than mainly with resident children. She focuses on some of the principles of family therapy and makes connections to work with children in a residential child care context.

In Chapter 7, Gluck describes a model of care in which residential staff approximate to family members. It is argued that the role in this context is not to provide a permanent substitute family, but to improve the attachment and skills of children so that they are better able to cope when returning to their families of origin.

Stevens in Chapter 8 briefly reviews demographic changes and the circumstances of children looked after in residential care to highlight the importance of stepfamily. She identifies typical patterns of family relationships, then builds a model of work for group care workers. The chapter provides details of particular techniques, including group work, games and story-telling which can enable young people and their families to work on issues related to family reconstitution.

In the following chapter, Chapter 9, Kosonen has analysed some of the key elements of sibling relationships, both in general and when children are separated. Based on a research study carried out by the author, the chapter contains much material and many quotations based on children's own perspectives. The implications for sustaining sibling relationships and working with relationship difficulties are then examined.

The penultimate chapter, Chapter 10, focuses on the significance of peer relationships for children in general. Deriving certain principles from empirical research, Hudson argues that group care can work with, rather than against, children's peer relationships, reorganising them as a source of support rather than necessarily as a negative influence. Attention is given to peer relationships within establishments, external to establishments and the connections between these two. The author proposes that a peer-based approach challenges the individual and family exclusivity of some approaches to child care.

Lessons from all the ten chapters have significant implications for strategic planning and management and delivery of residential child care provision. Underlying many of the dilemmas and tensions facing practitioners and managers are the issues of power, prejudice and dependence (CCETSW 1991).

These issues are not, of course, being claimed as unique to residential or group care for children and young people, as they arise in all social work service delivery, but they have been shown by research evidence (Clough 1987; Harder and Pringle 1997; OECD 1998) to be especially salient in this context. Therefore, it is important to consider these three notions in relation to residential child care in more detail as all the chapters in this book have touched upon some aspects of these issues.

Power

Children and their families in residential care settings frequently feel at the receiving end of a complex set of power relationships. Learning how to coordinate appropriate services and support for children and their families begins with recognising that they are partners in this process. A child and family centred approach implies that they are no longer 'managed' but, rather, participate in decisions and, as needed, are supported and assisted by professionals with accessing and coordinating services. The professional's role very often should be built on family strengths and acknowledgement of family preferences, but often that is not the reality. At the level of long-term planning for their future, young people tend to feel excluded from decision-making machinery; at the level of day-to-day decisions about rules, behaviour, etc. Further, young people sometimes feel at the mercy of arbitrary rules and ad hoc decision-making by staff (Fisher et al. 1989); and at the level of personal power in relationships, they have often been taken advantage of at home or elsewhere by exploitative sexual relationships, physical cruelty and in other ways.

Young people therefore feel powerless at many levels. The greatest, and often hidden, irony is that not only the child feels powerless, but so do the parent, the residential worker and the fieldwork professional too; they tend to feel that events and people are beyond their control, yet it is the young person who remains most vulnerable (Lindsay 1998).

Prejudice

In particular, children in residential care settings may have been at the receiving end of powerful actions stemming from various forms of prejudice, whether racist, sexist, class-based or due to disability. Whether experienced at home, at school, in the street or elsewhere for some, these experiences may be compounded by further prejudicial actions within the care setting: variations on this theme will include the predicaments of black and minority ethnic children in a setting where most staff and young people are white and where white images prevail and a subculture of racist remarks among the child's peers goes unchallenged by staff (Chakrabarti et al. 1998).

In addition, young women may live in a mixed-sex adolescent residential unit where male macho images and activities perpetuate stereotypes which tend to attack or undermine young women's self-image and self-respect.

Another version of the prejudice which tends to disadvantage children, young people and their families in group care is the stigma associated with being seen to live in residential care or to attend a centre. This stigma is often increased by public labelling of buildings and vehicles, and may be reinforced by bureaucratic structures such as bulk ordering of food and the order-book purchase of clothes. While many units have attempted to move away from these more obvious forms of stigma, it sometimes seems that, whatever measures are taken by staff to reduce it, the stigma felt by the young person is experienced as profoundly damaging to self-respect.

Furthermore, many professionals themselves contribute to this stigma by continuing to view group care as a last resort, to be used only when all else has failed; such an attitude needs to be challenged during training, since it so easily becomes a self-fulfilling prophecy.

Dependence

Childhood is a gradual and often, for some, painful journey from absolute dependence to relative independence, and for many children and young people in group care the experience of dependence has been profoundly traumatic. They have neither felt safe or happy with the parents or others upon whom they have had to depend, nor have they stayed long enough in any one setting to achieve any lasting dependence; in some situations they have had unrealistic levels of independence expected of them at far too early an age.

Thus many children come into care settings ambivalent about dependence and therefore have great difficulty in accepting care and concern from those trying to help and support them. This situation is further complicated by the uncertainty and ambivalence which many professionals feel about how involved with one's clients it is appropriate to become.

Dependence has different, but no less powerful, connotations in a day-care as compared with a residential setting. For example, who is really in charge of the children in a family centre: the parents or the staff? The scenario is further complicated by the issues of power and prejudice outlined above, because the people upon whom the child is dependent also tend to be those perceived as holding the greater power; indeed, it is the power which could engender the dependence.

All the contributors in this book, on the basis of their experience of working with young people and their families, have indicated that good health care, education and family support are essential services to safeguard and promote children's welfare and strengthen the capacity of families under stress to meet the needs of their children.

The issues and dilemmas that affect young people at risk and their families cannot be effectively tackled, let alone solved, without a coordinated and lifelong approach which emphasises people-to-people relationships, working 'with' rather than 'for' them. The failure of some services to meet needs of young people and their families, and the realisation that many child and family care issues need to be treated holistically, have resulted in the need for integrated services. The chapters in this book have attempted to provide examples of what these services may look like, the context in which they may function and how they may operate. It also has identified some of the challenges still to be met.

References

Cadman, M. and Chakrabarti, M. (1999) 'Child poverty and deprivation in the industrialised countries: A review.' *Journal of Economic Studies 26*, 1, 58–72.

Central Council for Education and Training in Social Work (CCETSW) (1991) *The Teaching of Child Care in the Diploma in Social Work.* London: CCETSW.

Chakrabarti, M., Thorne, J., Hosie, A., Lindsay, M., Brown, J., Hill, M., and Khan, I. *et al.* (1998) *Valuing Diversity.* Edinburgh: The Stationery Office.

Fisher, M., Marsh, P., Phillips, D. with Sainsbury, E. (1989) *In and Out of Care: The Experiences of Children, Parents and Social Workers.* London: Batsford BAAF.

Ford, R. and Chakrabarti, M. (eds) (1988) *Welfare Abroad.* Edinburgh: Scottish Academic Press.

Harder, M. and Pringle, K. (1997) *Protecting Children in Europe.* Aalborg: Aalborg University Press.

Lindsay, M. (1998) 'Moving mountains armed only with a teaspoon: The work of a centre of excellence for residential child care.' *Social Work Education 17*, 3, 339–349.

Organisation for Economic Cooperation and Development (OECD) (1998) *Children and Families at Risk.* Paris: OECD.

Rampakash, D. (1994) 'Poverty in the countries of the European Union: A synthesis of Eurostat's statistical research on poverty.' *Journal of European Social Policy 4*, 2.

Titmuss, R. (1979) *Commitment to Welfare.* London: Allen & Unwin.

Trevillion, S. (1997) 'The globalisation of European social work.' *Social Work in Europe 4*, 1.

The Contributors

William Carty is a child and youth worker and director of residential services, The George Hull Centre for Children and Families, a large children's mental health centre. He is an instructor in the School of Child and Youth Work, Humber College, Toronto, Canada.

Mono Chakrabarti is Professor of Social Work at the University of Strathclyde in Scotland. He has published in the fields of comparative social policy, community care and anti-racism.

Nova Fariss is Director of Mofflyn, a caring agency of the Uniting Church in Western Australia. Having graduated in social work in 1973, she has worked in statutory and non-statutory agencies in Western Australia and the Northern Territory. Her areas of practice have included community development, program development, child protection, out-of-home care, and services to people with disabilities. She is also an active participant in the state and national peak bodies in these fields.

Nechama Gluck is a senior educational and developmental psychologist. In the 'Mifal' she is chief psychologist, a member of the managing directorate and supervises psychologists and expressive therapists.

Fr Denis Halliday spent his life working to improve the lives of families in which disruption had occurred because of activities and difficulties experienced by their sons. He was ordained in 1973 as a Salesian Priest and subsequently spent 18 years at Boys' Town, Engadine, NSW Australia – partly as director. He held a masters degree in social work and was well known for his contributions to the profession over many years. While engaged in research to complete requirements for a PhD at the Australian Catholic University, he was diagnosed with motor neurone disease and died in July 1997 before he was able to complete his project.

Malcolm Hill is Director of the Centre for the Child and Society at the University of Glasgow. After working for ten years in social services departments, he has undertaken teaching and research with respect to children and families since 1979. He became Professor of Social Work at the University of Glasgow in 1996.

John Hudson is a Freelance Management Consultant for the Health and Personal Social Services. He is based in Huddersfield in England.

Marjut Kosonen, originally from Finland, obtained her CQSW and M.Phil in social work and social administration in 1977 at the University of York. She has worked as a child care social worker, manager and planner in the UK. She is currently responsible for the registration and inpsection services in Angus Council in Scotland and a post-graduate student at the Centre for the Study of Child at the University of Glasgow.

Elizabeth Ridgely is Executive Director of the George Hull Centre for Children and Families and Director of the Family Therapy Training Program. She is adjunct Professor of Social Work Practice and lecturer in the Department of Psychiatry at the University of Toronto, Canada.

Irene Stevens works for the National Autistic Society as Head of Social Work Services at Daldorch House Residential School. She qualified as a social worker in 1982 and worked at the short-stay adolescent refuge in Airdrie, Scotland for six years. After spending two years as senior groupworker in Priesthill, Glasgow, she moved to Falkirk College as senior lecturer in social care. She then worked at John Wheatley College, Glasgow, as Head of School for Community Services and Care.

Andrew Turnbull works as a services manager with Perth and Kinross Council social work services. Before coming to Perth in 1988, he worked in residential care, fieldwork, teaching and support services.

Subject Index

Author Index